W9-BWW-419

FACTS AT YOUR FINGERTIPS

ENDANGERED ANIMALS
MAMMALS OF THE SOUTHERN HEMISPHERE

BROWN BEAR BOOKS

Published by Brown Bear Books Limited

4877 N. Circulo Bujia
Tucson, AZ 85718
USA

and

First Floor
9-17 St. Albans Place
London N1 ONX
UK

© 2011 Brown Bear Books Ltd

Library of Congress Cataloging-in-Publication Data

Mammals of the Southern Hemisphere / edited by Tim Harris.
   p. cm. – (Facts at your fingertips. endangered animals)
 Includes bibliographical references and index.
 Summary: "Describes various mammals in the Southern
Hemisphere that are endangered and at risk of becoming extinct.
Data Sheet sidebars and maps accompany the text"–Provided by
publisher.
 ISBN 978-1-936333-35-6 (library binding)
1. Rare mammals–Southern Hemisphere–Juvenile literature. 2.
Endangered species–Juvenile literature. I. Harris, Tim. II. Title. III.
Series.

 QL706.8.M25 2012
 599.16809181'4–dc22

                          2010053970

ISBN-13 978-1-936333-35-6

Editorial Director: Lindsey Lowe
Editor: Tim Harris
Creative Director: Jeni Child
Designer: Lynne Lennon
Children's Publisher: Anne O'Daly
Production Director: Alastair Gourlay

Printed in the United States of America

In this book you will see the following key at top left of
each entry. The key shows the level of threat faced by each
animal, as judged by the International Union for the
Conservation of Nature (IUCN).

EX	Extinct
EW	Extinct in the Wild
CR	Critically Endangered
EN	Endangered
VU	Vulnerable
NT	Near Threatened
LC	Least Concern
O	Other (this includes Data Deficient and Not Evaluated)

For a few animals that have not been evaluated since 2001,
the old status of Lower Risk still applies and this is shown by
the letters **LR** on the key.

For more information on Categories of Threat, see pp. 54–57.

Picture Credits

Abbreviations: c=center; t=top; l=left; r=right.

Cover Images

Front: *Orang-Utan*, Thinkstock/Comstock
Back: *Cheetah*, Thinkstock/Digital Vision

AL: Andrea Florence 18–19; Chris Harvey 5; Edwin Mickelburgh 61;
AP: Jean-Paul Ferrero 51; **BCC:** Gunter Ziesler 16–17; **Dave Watts:**
49, 53; **FLPA:** H. Clark 6t; Frants Hartmann 57; **IUCN:** 59; NHPA:
A.N.T. 47; **PEP:** Martin Rugner 14–15; **Photolibrary:** Kathie Atkinson
42–43, Alan and Sandy Carey 10–11, 35, Martin Colbeck 28–29,
Marty Cordano 56, Daniel J. Cox 09, 25, 31, Tui De Roy 22–23, 58,
Michael Dick/Animals Animals 27, John Downer 38–39, Nick
Gordon 12–13, Howard Hall 6b, 20–21, David Haring 35 insert,
Mike Hill 36–37, Hilary Pooley 8–9, Norbert Rosing 58–59, Konrad
Wothe 33. **Thinkstock:** Digital Vision 1, Photos.com 54–55

Artwork © Brown Bear Books Ltd

*Brown Bear Books has made every attempt to contact the copyright
holder. If you have any information please email
smortimer@brownbearbooks.co.uk*

CONTENTS

What is a Mammal?

Mammals typically have a high body temperature, usually about 95 to 100°F (35 to 38°C). They are homeothermic, meaning that this temperature is normally kept fairly constant throughout the animal's life. Mammals are also referred to as endotherms, meaning that the warmth is generated internally, making them largely independent of external sources of heat such as the warmth of the sun. Their offspring are born as active babies and fed on milk secreted by the mammary glands of the mother. Echidnas (pp. 50–51) and the platypus (pp. 52–53) are exceptional in producing eggs, but still nourishing their young with milk.

Parental care, which sometimes lasts for years, is normal among mammals and allows the offspring to learn from older animals. Generally, families are small, and the young are well looked after to achieve a higher survival rate. Many species also live in social groups in which individuals cooperate to raise their young more successfully. Most mammals have a hairy or furry coat, which helps insulate them and maintain their high body temperature. Some—whales, for example—are nearly hairless as an adaptation to their particular way of life, but insulation is then provided by large amounts of fat (blubber) under the skin. In conjunction with their warm body mammals also have a very efficient blood circulatory system. It works faster and at higher pressures than in all other animals except birds. Endothermic homeothermy (warm-bloodedness) and an efficient blood system enable muscles and nerves to work faster, speed up digestion of food, help babies grow more rapidly, and generally assist mammals in living a much more active life than most other creatures.

Variations on a Theme

The basic mammal body plan, including four feet each with five toes, has been modified to allow the development of highly efficient diggers, runners, swimmers, and fliers. The teeth are also specialized to cope with many different kinds of food, from meat to nuts, leaves, fish, grass, blood, and insects.

These characteristic features of mammals enable them to live in a wide variety of habitats more independently of their surroundings (air temperature, for example) than any other animals. Mammals occur on all the continents—in the polar regions, deserts, mountaintops, and jungles. Some can make prolonged dives into deep oceans. Mammals can survive successfully in a wider diversity of habitats than any other animal group of comparable size. One species (our own) has even left this world to visit another—no other animal ever did that!

Mammals and People

Some mammals have become very abundant and widespread. Many (such as horses, dogs, cattle, and sheep) have also played a key role in the success of our own species, helping humans in their conquest of the planet by providing us with meat, milk, leather, transportation, and muscle power. Some assist in medical research to aid our own species, but others are significant pests and carriers of disease.

The History of Mammals

The first mammals evolved when dinosaurs ruled the world, about 100 million years ago. Mammals are therefore a comparatively new group of animals; many others have a much more ancient origin. Reptiles, for example, first appeared over 200 million years earlier. The first mammals were small and insignificant creatures that looked like today's solenodons and gymnures. From simple beginnings mammals have evolved into a wide assortment of species based on shared features and now include the blue whale (pp. 22–23), the largest animal ever. The smallest mammal

The earliest mammals *were small, inconspicuous insect-eaters like the long-extinct Megazostrodon (above). Over the last 200 million years mammals have come to dominate the planet, and now the group includes animals as diverse as bats, kangaroos, elephants (left), and human beings.*

own survival or a danger to domestic animals. Large mammals are also in danger simply because of their size. Elephants, for example, take up a lot of space and need a great deal of food every day. An African elephant (pp. 36–37) might eat the same amount as, say, two cows, but the same vegetation cannot feed both. The same patch of ground cannot grow grass and leaves for elephants and other large wild mammals, while at the same time producing crops for people. Often the expansion of farmland has pushed wild animals back into less suitable areas, and their numbers have dwindled. Sometimes the wild mammals, large and small, are forced to steal from the crops planted on the land they used to occupy. They are then called pests and eliminated with guns, traps, and poisons. Even using more humane forms of control, such as putting up fences instead of killing the animals, forces them to live in smaller areas that

is the Etruscan shrew; at about 2 grams it is smaller than many beetles. Over the last one to two million years enormous changes have taken place in the variety of mammal species present in different parts of the world. Many have become extinct or been reduced to critically small numbers.

Why Are Mammals at Risk?

In historic times mammals have suffered heavily from attacks by humans, particularly the larger species and those perceived to be fiercer (such as the cheetah, pp. 8–9, leopard, pp. 10–11, and mountain gorilla, pp. 30–31) that were considered to be a threat to our cannot support such high numbers. It is the larger species that have suffered most simply because they need large amounts of space, just as we do. Get rid of an elephant herd, and it creates room for 100 people and their crops. As numbers of humans have increased, wild mammals have been pushed aside. For example, during a 30-year period when elephants declined drastically in Kenya, the high human birthrate there meant that the lost elephants were replaced by almost exactly the same total tonnage of people.

Domestic mammals such as cattle, sheep, and goats have everywhere increased in numbers, replacing their wild relatives and competing for the limited amounts of available food.

Exploitation

Some wild mammals have been specially hunted for their skins (ocelot, for example), meat (banteng), or other products (such as wool from vicuñas, ivory from African elephants, pp. 36–37, or blubber from whales, pp. 20–25). Overexploitation has led to catastrophic population declines. This particularly affects the larger species because they do not breed rapidly, having few young and taking a long time to

reach breeding age. Populations cannot cope with large numbers being killed, and they collapse. Larger mammals also tend to live longer, often more than 20 years. That allows time for poisons and other pollutants (such as heavy metals and polychlorinated biphenyls, known as PCBs) to accumulate and take effect, preventing breeding and causing sickness and sometimes even death. The accumulation of poisons is less of a problem for animals that naturally live for only a short time.

Some mammals (such as whales and many large land species) are thinly spread over a wide area. Their distribution therefore suggests a level of abundance that is misleading. They seem to be common, but widespread populations that are thin on the ground are vulnerable to fragmentation. Once the population is broken into small groups, they often include too few to be viable, and they die out one after another. Some

The lack of natural food sources *as a result of habitat disturbance can result in young being abandoned and conservationists intervening. Here bats are fed from a syringe on goats' milk.*

The lifeless body *of a gray whale, washed up on a beach after it was ensnared in a discarded fishing net. Accidental deaths—ranging from roadkills to incidents such as this—claim the lives of mammals the world over.*

Percentage of mammals threatened
- 0–7
- 7–12
- 12–17
- 17–100

Southern hemisphere *countries that have the highest percentage of threatened mammals (above) include Australia, Madagascar, and Indonesia.*

species are at risk from interbreeding with their domesticated relatives, creating hybrids.

Smaller Species

Small mammals have problems too. Their size makes them vulnerable to predators and to cold weather. At least half of all known mammal species are rat-sized or smaller. One-third of all mammals are rodents (rats, mice, squirrels, and so on), and one in five is a bat. These animals are often difficult to study and are normally largely ignored. This means that we simply do not know what their real status is. Their numbers are unknown and not monitored. Many may go extinct without ever being officially recorded as being present.

These are special problems for mammals; but like other animals, the mammals also suffer from habitat destruction. Those that are adapted to a particular way of life suffer heavily from the cutting down of trees or the mass removal of their food (such as fish) to feed humans. This is a particular problem where populations are small to start with.

Numbers of Threatened Species in Each of the Major Mammalian Groups	
Rodents (mice, squirrels, and beavers)	461
Bats	253
Carnivores (dogs, cats, bears, and otters)	98
Primates (monkeys, apes, and lemurs)	224
Ungulates (horses, rhinos, hippos, deer, and antelope)	149
Marsupials	61

Rodents, *which constitute 30 percent of all mammals, represent the highest number of threatened species (above).*

The Situation Today

There are about 5,500 species of mammal (but more than 10,000 species of birds and almost 40,000 fish). About 80 to 90 mammal species have become extinct in the last 300 years, and many subspecies and local varieties are also extinct or nearly so. Of the living species about 3.4 percent are now Critically Endangered, 8.2 percent Endangered, and 9.0 percent Vulnerable. More than one-quarter of all known mammals are threatened in some way. That is about twice the proportion of threatened birds. The highest proportion of endangerment is among the primates: 49 percent of primate species are threatened.

Cheetah

Acinonyx jubatus

The cheetah is well known for its lean body, great speed, and spotted coat. Years of persecution have made it one of the world's most vulnerable big cats.

The world's fastest land animal over short distances, the cheetah is also the most ancient of all the big cats. Cheetahs probably evolved on the plains of the Middle East four million years ago. Fossil evidence shows that 10,000 years ago cheetahs roamed in places as far apart as North America, Europe, Asia, and Africa. The cheetah's heyday lasted until the last ice age; since then human populations have exploded, and the cheetah's range and numbers have shrunk. In their ancestral homeland of the Middle East the Asian subspecies of cheetah is Critically Endangered, with very few, if any, animals left in remote parts of Iran and Afghanistan. The situation is only slightly better in Africa.

Cheetahs differ from other big cats in their adaptations for hunting. The shape of a cheetah—a narrow, elongated body and long, muscular legs—is ideal for sprinting. Unlike its cousins, the cheetah cannot completely retract its claws; it needs them to provide extra grip when running at high speeds. Cheetahs take advantage of the fact that other large predators rest during the hottest part of the day and do their hunting in the late morning and early afternoon. A cheetah first stalks its prey, then runs it down at speeds of up to 60 miles per hour (95 km/h). The flexibility of the cat's long spine allows it to take huge strides. Most chases are over in about 20 seconds—any prey that can evade capture for more than a minute will probably escape since the cheetah cannot maintain its speed for long.

Cheetahs kill by clamping their jaws around the victim's throat. This has the effect of closing off the windpipe, so the prey stops breathing. The cheetah does not have particularly big teeth, but exceptionally large nostrils ensure that, even when out of breath from the chase, it can inhale deeply through its nose while maintaining a suffocating grip with its jaws.

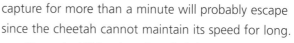

DATA PANEL

Cheetah

Acinonyx jubatus

Family: Felidae

World population: 7,000–10,000

Distribution: Sub-Saharan Africa, excluding Congo Basin; most of South Africa; Iran

Habitat: Grasslands

Size: Length head/body: 44–60 in (112–152 cm); tail: 20–33 in (51–84 cm); height at shoulder: 25–37 in (64–94 cm); males slightly larger than females. Weight: 86–143 lb (39–65 kg)

Form: Slender big cat with long, muscular legs, small head, and long, curved tail. Coat golden yellow with black spots; small, rounded ears; black stripes either side of nose

Diet: Mainly gazelles; also impala, warthogs, small antelopes, gamebirds, and hares

Breeding: Between 1 and 8 young (average 3–5) born at any time of year (peak births March–June). Life span 12–14 years in the wild; up to 17 years in captivity

Related endangered species: No close relatives

Status: IUCN VU; Asian subspecies *A. jubatus venaticus* CR

A **cheetah** *can achieve speeds of 0 to 45 miles per hour (0 to 72 km/h) in 2.5 seconds—acceleration to rival some sports cars.*

Cheetah means "spotted one" in Hindi, and every cheetah has markings as unique as a fingerprint. In some Zimbabwean cheetahs the spots along the back and tail join up to form a blotchy pattern. Animals with this distinctive pattern are called king cheetahs and they were once thought to be a separate subspecies. However, it has been shown that they are simply part of the natural variation within the local population. The black "tear stripes" on the cheetah's face are thought to help protect their eyes from sunlight reflecting off their cheeks. Human athletes imitate this idea when they daub paint across their cheeks and noses.

Cheetahs breed at any time of year. A female is in heat and ready to mate every 12 days unless she already has cubs. She will give birth to three to five cubs per litter; but infant mortality is high, and fewer than one-third of all cubs survive to adulthood. Small, widely scattered cheetah populations mean that much inbreeding occurs, and many cubs are born with genetic defects. A solution might be to release some animals from captivity, bringing in fresh genetic stock.

Tourist Attraction

Cheetahs face problems even in protected national parks. Tourists want to see the cheetahs wherever possible, and this tends to scare off prey and distracts the animals from hunting. Disturbance of cheetah kills also allows scavengers such as jackals to nip in and steal the food. Cheetahs are not good at defending themselves from this sort of interference.

Leopard

Panthera pardus

The adaptable leopard is a very widespread species and is still quite common in some parts of Africa. However, elsewhere hunting for fur, persecution by farmers, and loss of habitat have brought several subspecies to the brink of extinction.

Leopards are the most adaptable of the big cats. They can live in a wide variety of climates and habitat types, so long as they have a plentiful supply of food and secure cover in which to hide their food, rear their young, and rest during the day. Prey can be anything from large antelopes and pigs to rats, rabbits, and birds, and if times are really hard, insects.

The leopard can live in forests or open spaces and at altitudes ranging from sea level to well over 16,000 feet (5,000 m). Leopards from different places often differ in appearance, none so much as the black panther, an all black or "melanistic" leopard that inhabits dark, humid forests in Southeast Asia. Regional differences are not always this obvious; but because leopards from one population are usually isolated from those elsewhere, they are recognized as distinct subspecies.

As one would expect for such a generalist predator able to cope with extremes of climate, the leopard's distribution is large. In fact, it has the widest range of any cat. Leopards once thrived in areas ranging from the baking savannas of South Africa to the lofty Himalayas, from the Javan rain forests to windswept Siberian plateaus. They are still present in these places, but in all but their African stronghold the species is in serious trouble.

Panthera
pardus
panthera

DATA PANEL

Leopard

Panthera pardus

Family: Felidae

World population: Probably considerably fewer than the 700,000 estimated in 1988

Distribution: Largest populations in sub-Saharan Africa, with scattered and shrinking populations in northern Africa, the Middle East, Pakistan, India, Bangladesh, Sri Lanka, China, Siberia, Korea, Indochina, and Indonesia

Habitat: Very diverse; includes forests, grasslands, and deserts, lowlands and mountains; anywhere where there is sufficient food and cover, such as trees, scrub, or rocks

Size: Length head/body: 35–75 in (90–190 cm); tail 22–42 in (58–110 cm); height to shoulder: 17.5–31 in (45–78 cm); males up to 50% bigger than females. Weight: 61–200 lb (28–90 kg)

Form: Large, pale-buff to deep-chestnut cat marked with rosettes of dark on body and tail; head marked with smaller spots, belly and legs with large blotches; very dark or black individuals are known as black panthers

Diet: Mostly hoofed animals such as gazelles, wildebeest, deer, goats, and pigs, including livestock; also takes monkeys, rodents, rabbits, birds, and invertebrates

Breeding: Between 1 and 6 (usually 2 or 3) cubs born after gestation of 13–15 weeks at any time of year in Africa, more seasonal elsewhere; weaned at 3 months; mature at 3 years; may live over 20 years

Related endangered species: Asiatic lion (*Panthera leo persica*) CR; tiger (*P. tigris*) EN; snow leopard (*Uncia uncia*) EN; lion (*P. leo*) VU; jaguar (*P. onca*) NT

Status: IUCN NT, but some subspecies more seriously threatened. Isolated Javan leopard (*Panthera pardus melas*), for example, is CR

Changing Circumstances

The problems for leopards in different parts of the species' range vary so widely that the IUCN places different regional subspecies in different categories of threat. In sub-Saharan Africa leopards are still relatively numerous, especially inside national parks such as the Serengeti. Here the protection the leopards receive and the abundant prey available to them mean that they are doing very well.

The leopard is legally protected in almost every country in its range, although several nations permit limited hunting and licenses for hunting and export of skins, and mounted trophies are granted on a regular basis. The licenses are restricted by country and usually account for between 1,000 and 2,000 leopards a year. This level of hunting is probably sustainable and an improvement on the situation in the 1960s and 1970s, when over 50,000 leopards were killed a year.

Legal hunting may not be the threat it once was, but outside protected habitats (which account for only about 13 percent of the species' range) leopards are suffering from habitat loss, persecution, and poaching. Five subspecies, from northwestern Africa, the Middle East, Siberia, and Korea are listed as Critically Endangered, with populations of fewer than 250 animals and in one case as few as 17. Four other subspecies, from the Middle East, Southeast Asia, and Indonesia are listed as Endangered.

Unlike other big cats, leopards do not seem to mind living alongside people. When areas of natural habitat are settled and turned over to agriculture, the adaptable leopard does not automatically move on. Many will stick around and adjust their behavior to make the best living they can under the circumstances. Some leopards attack livestock, and others even become man-eaters, so most governments permit the shooting of problem leopards. Man-eating leopards seem to be a particular problem in India, where dozens of people are killed by leopards every year.

The leopard's *coat serves to break up its outline, especially in dappled sunlight. This camouflage is useful for hunting and allows the big cat to rest undetected in the branches of a tree during the day.*

Jaguar

Panthera onca

The jaguar is the most accomplished climber of all the big cats and is almost equally at home prowling the forest floor or swimming in rivers and pools. However, its adaptability is no protection against the erosion of its forest habitat or other human activities that threaten its existence.

The jaguar is the largest cat in the Americas and the only member of the big cat genus *Panthera* to be found in this region. It bears a resemblance to the leopard and is often thought of as the South American equivalent. Its coat pattern consists of black markings on a golden-tan background. Entirely black jaguars, known as black panthers, are relatively common, the all-black or melanistic condition being caused by a single gene that overrides those for normal patterning. A cub needs to inherit only a single copy of the melanistic gene from either of its parents to be born with a jet black coat. Albino jaguars have also been recorded, but they are extremely rare.

The jaguar is more heavily built than its African cousin, the leopard. Its head and jaws are substantially larger and more powerful, an arrangement that hints at its preferred method of finishing off its prey—with a crushing bite to the skull. The jaguar is the most accomplished climber among the big cats and will often ambush prey from trees. Prey includes almost anything it can catch; over 85 different species have been recorded in its diet. Nevertheless, the jaguar prefers larger mammals such as peccaries (a kind of wild pig), tapirs, and deer, though in dense rainforest where these are hard to come by, it often turns instead to fish and reptiles. It is an excellent swimmer, and with its powerful jaw and stout canine teeth it can crack open the tough shells of turtles. Indeed, it has been suggested that this ability to attack reptilian prey is one reason the jaguar survived in the New World during the Pleistocene period, when a significant proportion of large herbivore prey became

extinct. In places where human settlements spread into their territory, jaguars often take livestock. In Brazil domestic cows are the main diet of many jaguars living near cattle ranches.

The jaguar would certainly be capable of killing a human; but when people have reported being "stalked" through the forest, it is likely that the jaguar was merely making sure the trespassers were leaving its territory. If it really had intended to eat the people, they would surely not have lived to tell the tale!

Jaguars can probably breed all year round, but most births take place when prey is most abundant. The two sexes only tolerate each other when courting or mating; the male has nothing to do with the raising of offspring. Only when mating does the jaguar make much noise—a deep, throaty cry is the closest it ever gets to a roar.

Cubs are born in litters of one to four, with twins being most common. The young are blind at birth and will not leave the den until they are two weeks old. The mother moves her cubs much like other cats, grasping them by the scruff of the neck. The cubs spend a lot of time playing together, and the mother is remarkably tolerant of their boisterous games, which more often than not involve clambering all over

her, biting her tail, and pulling her ears! The cubs remain with the mother until she is ready to breed again, which can be as long as two years.

Threats to Survival

Jaguars were once widely hunted for their skins, which made valuable fur coats, but the trade was banned in the 1970s. Nowadays the main threat comes from cattle ranchers, who shoot jaguars that kill their livestock and may also hunt them for sport. Even more of a threat is the destruction of forests to make way for other animals. Continuous grazing by cattle and sheep prevents new trees from growing, and the vast prairies that are formed are unsuitable for the forest-dwelling jaguar.

A jaguar cub. *The animal's relatively short limbs are an adaptation for climbing; jaguars are the most arboreal of the big cats.*

DATA PANEL

Jaguar

Panthera onca

Family: Felidae

World population: Unknown, but probably in low thousands

Distribution: From Mexico to Patagonia, including Belize, Panama, Costa Rica, Guatemala, Honduras, Nicaragua, Surinam, Colombia, Ecuador, Guyana, Venezuela, French Guiana, Peru, Brazil, Bolivia, Uruguay, Paraguay, Argentina. Formerly southwestern U.S.

Habitat: Tropical forests, swamps, rivers, pools, and open country

Size: Length head/body: 44–72 in (112–185 cm); tail: 18–30 in (46–76 cm); females smaller than males.

Weight: 100–250 lb (45–123 kg)

Form: Robust-looking big cat. Golden coat with black rings, rosettes, and dots; pale underside

Diet: Wild pigs, capybaras, tapirs, domestic cattle, horses, fish, frogs, turtles, tortoises, and young alligators

Breeding: Cubs born in litters of 1–4 at any time of year. Life span up to 12 years in the wild; up to 22 years recorded in captivity

Related endangered species: Other big cats, including the Asiatic lion (*Panthera leo persica*) CR and tiger (*P. tigris*) EN

Status: IUCN NT

Spectacled Bear

Tremarctos ornatus

The tree-dwelling spectacled bear is one of the larger residents of the mysterious Andean cloud forests. Its habitat is shrinking at an alarming rate.

It is easy to understand how the spectacled bear got its name: The whitish rings round its eyes are very distinctive. It is the largest member of the Carnivora in South America and is a direct descendant of the bulldog bear, which 10,000 years ago was the largest predator in the Americas. The spectacled bear is a powerful animal, and there are records of individuals killing and eating cattle. However, they feed mainly on fruit and other vegetable materials. Meat rarely amounts to more than 5 percent of the diet and is mostly in the form of insects and carrion.

Spectacled bears live in the cloud forest of the Andean mountains. Dense vegetation thrives in the damp atmosphere. Much of the interior remains unexplored, and relatively little is known about the lives of the spectacled bears. The bears appear to spend most of their time in the trees, where they clamber around up to 50 feet (15 m) above the ground, looking for fruit. They are especially partial to bromeliads, young palm fronds and figs but will seek out any sweet, energy-rich food.

Spectacled bears do not hibernate because they do not have to contend with seasonal changes in food availability. Their diet may change as different plants come into season, but at no time is there any shortage, so the bears remain active all year.

Spectacled bears mate between April and June, and pregnancies last between five and eight months. It is likely that the variation occurs because, once mated, female spectacled bears can put their pregnancy on hold: a strategy known as delayed implantation. Only when conditions seem right for the pregnancy to proceed successfully will the embryo be implanted and continue to develop. (This is speculation, but a similar process happens in polar and grizzly bears, so it is likely to occur in spectacled bears too.)

DATA PANEL

Spectacled bear

Tremarctos ornatus

Family: Ursidae

World population: Probably more than 5,000

Distribution: Andean mountains in northern Bolivia, Colombia, Ecuador, Peru, and Venezuela

Habitat: Cloud forests on lower Andean slopes

Size: Length: 4.2–6.2 ft (1.3–1.9 m); height at shoulder on all fours: 30 in (76 cm); females smaller than males. Weight: 175–385 lb (80–175 kg)

Form: A short-legged, brownish-black, largely arboreal bear with variable pale markings on the face and chest

Diet: Mostly plant material, including fruit, sugarcane, and corn; some small mammals, birds, and carrion

Breeding: One or 2 young (occasionally 3 in captivity) born November–February. Life span may exceed 25 years

Related endangered species: Sloth bear *(Melursus ursinus)* VU; polar bear *(Ursus maritimus)* VU; Asiatic black bear *(U. thibetanus)* VU

Status: IUCN VU

Cubs are born between November and February, about six weeks before the peak fruiting period of local plants. There is plenty of food available just when the new family needs it most. The newborn cubs are blind and very small, weighing no more than 18 ounces (500 g) each. After a month they are ready to begin exploring with their mother. She spends six to eight months teaching them to fend for themselves, after which they will be on their own.

Shrinking Populations

The spectacled bear faces many problems. Its habitat is shrinking at a rapid rate as the forests are cleared for timber production and agriculture. This brings the bears into contact with human activities, reducing survival. Although the bear is legally protected, there is a thriving trade in body parts, especially skins, meat, and fat. The paws are valued too, being thought to have medicinal properties. Hunting and international trade in spectacled bears is banned, but legislation is difficult to enforce. In Peru the wild bear population is so small that inbreeding is becoming a problem: Scientists have already noted a decrease in the size of bears and the size of their litters.

Spectacled bears *are the largest carnivores in South America, though meat only accounts for 5 percent of their diet. Despite their bulk, they can climb trees with ease.*

Giant Otter

Pteronura brasiliensis

Formerly conspicuous and widespread, the giant otter is now extinct in parts of its range. Its decline is mainly a direct result of excessive and uncontrolled hunting.

The giant otter is more sociable than many otter species. It lives in family groups of up to 20 individuals, although most groups are made up of between six to eight animals. There is usually a mated pair, along with their most recently born young, and some offspring from the previous year. Unlike the more familiar river otters of North America and Europe, the group stays close together, and the adult male and female often share the same den.

Giant otters eat what they can get and cooperate with each other when hunting prey by driving shoals of fish into shallow water where they can be caught easily. They use their sensitive whiskers (vibrissae) to detect water turbulence caused by fish and other potential prey and pursue their victim underwater, catching it in their jaws. Otters often take slow-moving species, such as catfish, and will eat fish over 2 feet (60 cm) long. They wait for their partners to finish eating before moving on.

When ashore, giant otters mark out their riverbank territory with scent. One consequence of this is that it sends out a warning to other individuals or families in the area. Giant otters are also vocal, calling to each other with a wide range of squeals, barks, and whistles. Although useful for communication, such announcements make it easy for human hunters to locate and kill family groups.

Unlike many other mustelids, which are active under cover of darkness, giant otters are mainly active during the day. Coming out in daylight hours exposes the animals to many dangers, particularly from hunters with spears or guns. Another potentially fatal behavioral trait is the otter's curiosity. The animals swim around with their heads held high out of the water and will often move toward intruders, or possibly dangerous situations, to investigate them more closely. Again, such behavior makes them easy prey, and hunters are usually able to kill others of the group who linger to see what has happened.

Hunted for Fur

As in other species of otter, the fur of the giant otter is extremely dense and helps protect the animal from getting chilled when in the water. The giant otter's fur is particularly distinctive, being short, glossy, and velvety. Such qualities make it especially attractive as a fashion fur. Often a hunter will be able to sell a skin for the equivalent of two to three month's honest wages. After processing, the skin is worth five times as much to the fur trade. Official figures from Peru show that every year in the 1950s, over 1,000 giant otter skins were exported; numbers fell sharply as the giant otter population collapsed, and the trade in their pelts

and other parts was finally banned in 1970. However, it is thought likely that poaching continues, with skins being sent for export through neighboring countries such as Colombia.

The opening up of huge areas of South American forest for logging has made previously remote otter retreats more accessible to developers and others. Although the species was formerly widespread throughout tropical South America, giant otters are now extinct or nearly so in Argentina, Uruguay, and much of southern Brazil, and they have gone from many other parts of their former range. Recovery of the population is no easy task since the animal's main food—the fish in the river—is in demand to feed people as well, and there are increasing problems of pollution. A particular problem is chemical pollution from gold extraction along rivers. Settlements along river banks also make it difficult for the otters to find undisturbed places for dens.

The giant otter *is the largest of the freshwater otter species, with a distinctive flattened tail. It is still fairly numerous in the Pantanal of Brazil and in parts of Peru.*

DATA PANEL

Giant otter

Pteronura brasiliensis

Family: Mustelidae

World population: Unknown, possibly 1,000–5,000

Distribution: Formerly found over much of tropical South America, south to Argentina. Probably extinct in Argentina and most of Paraguay

Habitat: Slow-moving rivers, creeks, and swamps within forested areas

Size: Length head/body: 36 58 in (86–140 cm); tail: 14–42 in (33–100 cm). Weight: males 57–75 lb (26–34 kg); females 48–57 lb (22–26 kg)

Form: Large otter with short, glossy-brown fur that appears black when wet. Often white or creamy nose and throat. Feet webbed; tail tapering and flattened with a flange along each edge

Diet: Mainly fish; also freshwater crabs and occasionally mammals

Breeding: Up to 5 young in a single litter per year, born after gestation of 65–70 days. Life span over 14 years in captivity

Related endangered species: Marine otter (*Lutra felina*) EN; southern river otter (*L. provocax*) EN; hairy-nosed otter (*L. sumatrana*) EN; European otter (*L. lutra*) NT; smooth-coated otter (*Lutrogale perspicillata*) VU

Status: IUCN EN

Amazon River Dolphin

Inia geoffrensis

The world's largest river and its tributaries are home to the boto, or Amazon river dolphin. Pollution, dam-building, and overfishing are all threatening the future of this animal.

The Amazon river dolphin's range is naturally broken up into three main stretches of water, separated by extensive or perilous rapids. For this reason some scientists think that there are three distinct subspecies living in the Orinoco River in Venezuela, the Madeira River in Bolivia, and the Brazilian Amazon. However, other biologists maintain that these populations are not as separate as they seem. Every year the rivers flood, allowing large fish—and maybe also some river dolphins—to swim over and around the rapids. When the waters subside again, the dolphins become trapped, at least until the rains the following year.

This phenomenon repeats itself on a smaller scale throughout the dolphin's range, with animals moving through submerged areas of forest during the flood period and sometimes getting stranded in small lakes for the duration of the dry season.

The Risks of Isolation

The cyclic ebb and flow of flood waters is fairly commonplace in the region, and the dolphins usually manage to survive a season or two in quite small lakes, as long as there are plenty of fish trapped along with them. Problems can arise, however, when the lakes are drained to irrigate crops, or if humans compete for the same fish prey as the dolphins. Once the fish in a lake are gone, no more can arrive to replace them until the forest becomes flooded again the following year.

While local activities such as fishing and irrigation threaten isolated groups of dolphins, the building of dams for hydroelectric power and flood control can damage whole populations. Dams create permanent barriers to the dolphins' passage, cutting off whole populations. These isolated groups can become inbred and vulnerable to disease and local disasters from which there is no escape either up- or downstream.

River dolphins are not normally hunted, largely because local legend has it that they harbor the souls of drowned people. The dolphins themselves are frequent victims of

DATA PANEL

Amazon river dolphin (boto, pink dolphin)

Inia geoffrensis

Family: Iniidae

World population: Unknown

Distribution: Orinoco and Amazon river systems, South America

Habitat: Rivers and flooded forest

Size: Length 5.6–10 ft (1.7–3 m). Weight: up to 350 lb (160 kg); males can be almost twice as heavy as females

Form: Large, bluish-gray to pink dolphin with long dorsal (back) ridge and large fins and tail flukes; small eyes, long snout with peglike teeth, and bulging cheeks and forehead

Diet: Mostly fish; some crustaceans and turtles

Breeding: Single calf born May–September after gestation of 10–11 months; weaned at 1 year or more; maturity depends on size rather than age. Life span 30 years or more

Related endangered species: Yangtze river dolphin (*Lipotes vexillifer*) CR; Ganges river dolphin (*Platanista gangetica*) EN; Indus river dolphin (*P. minor*) EN

Status: IUCN DD

accidental drowning
after becoming caught up in
the huge nets set by local fishermen to
take river fish. When this happens, the fishermen
are happy enough to make use of the
unplanned extra catch by using oil extracted
from the dolphins' bodies as a lubricant and
lamp fuel.

Contamination by Mercury

Like other top Amazon predators, including giant
otters, river dolphins often suffer from the effects of
mercury poisoning. Mercury is used to refine the gold
that is mined in the region, and as many as 340 tons
(300 tonnes) are released into the river every year.
There is also a certain amount of natural mercury
present in the soil, and deforestation is increasing the
rate at which it is washed into the river by rainfall.
Mercury combines with other chemicals to produce a
compound called methyl mercury, significant quantities
of which then build up in the bodies of river fish. Any
animal that eats a lot of contaminated fish ends up

**Amazon river
dolphins** *have pink
skin that contains a little dark pigment. After prolonged
activity the pink color becomes more pronounced as blood
rushes to the surface to help the animal cool down.*

ingesting enough methyl mercury to cause serious
damage, including birth deformities, muscle-wasting,
nerve damage, and failure of the immune system. In
humans the condition is known as Minimata disease,
after the port in Japan where it was first diagnosed
when a factory polluted the local water with mercury.
The problem is even more severe for river dolphins,
since everything they eat comes from the river.

Sperm Whale

Physeter macrocephalus

The extraordinary-looking sperm whale is something of a mystery. It has been hunted on and off for 300 years for its oil, but is now protected. The true extent of the damage done to the world's sperm whale population by hunting may never be known.

The sperm whale is a record breaker in more ways than one. Not only is it the world's largest living carnivorous animal, it also has the largest brain of any creature and is the deepest diving mammal. Thanks largely to the American author Herman Melville's novel *Moby Dick* (1851), it is also one of the best-known whales.

Sperm whales were first hunted in the early 18th century. What is striking about the original hunt is that, despite the huge danger and expense of hunting whales, so much of the animal was wasted. The meat, skin, and most of the bones were considered virtually worthless.

Valuable Products

One of the most valuable sperm whale products was ambergris, a gray, waxy substance that lines the whale's intestines. Its function may be to protect the animal from the bites of squid and other prey. Ambergris was widely used by the perfume industry as a fixative that helped perfumes retain their scent. Ironically, it is not necessary to kill the whales to get the ambergris, since lumps of it can be found floating in the sea or washed ashore, having been coughed up or excreted by the whales. Today many perfume makers use artificial fixatives, so this strange substance is worth much less.

Carved or decorated sperm whale teeth called scrimshaw can fetch a high price, but their value is more related to the quality of craftsmanship than the ivory itself. The true value of a dead sperm whale was always its oil. Gallons of oil could be extracted by melting down the sperm whale's blubber. In large individuals the blubber sometimes forms a layer under

DATA PANEL

Sperm whale (spermaceti whale, cachalot)

Physeter macrocephalus

Family: Physeteridae

World population: Estimates vary from 200,000 to 1.5 million

Distribution: Global; in all the world's oceans and many adjoining seas

Habitat: Mostly deep ocean

Size: Length: 36–60 ft (11–19 m). Weight: 17–55 tons (15–50 tonnes); males larger and up to 3 times heavier than females

Form: Large whale with vast, boxlike head up to one third of total length. Single S-shaped blowhole on left-hand-side of snout; skin dark bluish-gray, fading with age; often wrinkled and covered in scars; white markings around mouth. Body tapers from head to tail. Teeth only in lower jaw

Diet: Mostly squid; some octopus and fish, including sharks

Breeding: Single young born in fall after gestation of 14–16 months; weaned at 2 years; female first breeds at 8–13 years, male at 25–27 years due to social hierarchy. Life span up to 77 years

Related endangered species: No close relatives, but various dolphins and other toothed whales are threatened, including vaquita porpoise (*Phocoena sinus*) CR

Status: IUCN VU

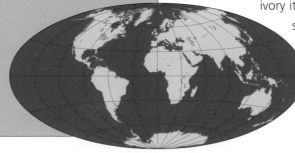

The sperm whale *gets its name from the oil-filled organ in its head—the spermaceti. No one is sure what the spermaceti does, but it may be used in the control of buoyancy or the production of sound.*

the skin up to 12 inches (30 cm) thick. The oil was used as a lubricant and in ointments and cosmetics. An additional 500 gallons (1,900 liters) of oil could be harvested from the spermaceti organ in a single whale's huge head. This was especially valuable since it was fine enough to be used to lubricate delicate machinery. It could also be turned into wax for making high-quality candles that burned cleanly with little soot. Spermaceti candles were popular in the late 18th and early 19th centuries, but were eventually replaced by kerosene lamps.

A Change in Hunting Practice

The sperm-whaling industry eventually declined. For almost a century the whales were not disturbed, and the world population stabilized. If hunting had not resumed in about 1930, it is estimated that there could be more than 3 million sperm whales in the world today.

The modern method of hunting is far more intensive. It peaked in the 1960s and 1970s, when 20,000 to 30,000 whales were slaughtered each year, five times as many as in the early 19th century. Although hunting is now banned, scientists still argue about the damage it actually did. Estimates of the current sperm whale population vary enormously, from just 200,000 to over one and a half million. One effect of hunting has been a shift in the sex ratio. Being much bigger, male sperm whales have always been targeted more than females. By the 1980s, when whaling ceased, there were more than twice as many females as males. It is feared that the imbalance may have led to increased inbreeding, which will damage the gene pool.

Blue Whale

Balaenoptera musculus

It took fewer than 50 years of intensive whaling to bring the largest animal the world has ever known to the brink of extinction. There are positive signs that the remaining blue whale population is beginning to make a recovery.

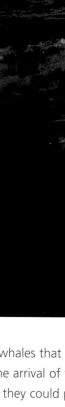

Humans have hunted whales for well over a thousand years, but it was not until the 1860s that new technology allowed whalers to hunt the largest species of all. Whaling in the late 19th century was difficult and dangerous; but by targeting the largest of the great whales, the whalers could reap enormous profits. Hunting for blue whales began in the North Atlantic; but as the populations there declined, attention turned to other oceans. In the early 1900s 90 percent of the world's quarter of a million blue whales lived in the Southern Hemisphere. When these rich hunting grounds were discovered, whaling stations were established on small islands in the Southern Ocean. At first whalers had to operate close to coastal factories and could not fully exploit the whales that remained far from land. However, with the arrival of the first factory ships in the mid-1920s, they could process their kills on the open ocean, and consequently the death toll soared.

By 1960 it became obvious that the blue whale was heading for extinction, but it was still several years before an international ban on commercial whaling was agreed. The intervening years cost the species several thousand more lives, bringing the total death toll to 350,000 in fewer than 70 years.

After the killing stopped there were high hopes that the blue whales would recover. By the mid-1980s there was evidence of a slight increase in numbers, and surveys showed that pregnancy rates had doubled, from about 25 percent in 1930 to over

DATA PANEL

Blue whale (great northern rorqual, sulphur-bottom)

Balaenoptera musculus

Family: Balaenidae

World population: 10,000–25,000

Distribution: Three separate populations: in the North Atlantic, North Pacific, and Southern Ocean respectively; the whales migrate annually between polar and tropical waters

Habitat: Deep oceans

Size: Length: 79–89 ft (24–27 m); occasionally up to 110 ft (33 m); females larger than males. Weight: 110–132 tons (100–120 tonnes); occasionally up to 209 tons (190 tonnes)

Form: Vast, streamlined body; bluish-gray skin with pale markings and white to yellow underside. Rounded snout; deep throat furrows; 2 blowholes with large splashguard; small dorsal fin set well back on body

Diet: Krill (planktonic shrimps) and other crustaceans

Breeding: Single young born after gestation of 10–12 months; weaned at 7–8 months; mature at 10 years. May live up to 110 years

Related endangered species: Fin whale *(Balaenoptera physalus)* EN; sei whale *(B. borealis)* EN; minke whale *(B. acutorostrata)* LC

Status: IUCN EN

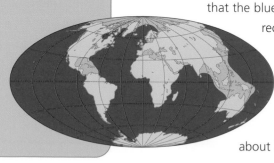

Blue whales *dive for about 10 to 20 minutes at a time before surfacing to take a dozen or so breaths, sending a spout of spray as high as 30 feet (9 m) into the air with each exhalation.*

50 percent. The total world population was estimated at the time at about 12,000 individuals. Early optimism may have proved premature but recent estimates suggest a world population of between 10,000 and 25,000.

Impoverished Oceans

The main reason why the whales' numbers have not recovered is simply because their habitat has altered for the worse. The annual catch of krill (planktonic shrimps) taken by the world's fisheries rose from practically nothing in the early 20th century to over 500,000 tons (455,000 tonnes) in 1986. An average blue whale needs about 7,700 pounds (3,500 kg) of krill a day to sustain its great bulk. Now that krill is fished on such a huge scale, there may simply not be enough food to meet the whales' requirements.

The seas are also more polluted now, and not just with chemicals. Toxins and biologically active substances that have been shown to damage other marine wildlife almost certainly affect large whales. In addition, whales are affected by noise pollution and alterations in local currents brought about by coastal developments. Large inland projects can also result in thousands of tons of silt being dumped at sea, making the water unsuitable for both whales and their food.

Humpback Whale

Megaptera novaeangliae

Having faced extinction in the 1960s, the humpback whale has responded well to protection. As long as the ban on whaling stays in place, it is set to become one of the world's best conservation success stories.

Over the past two or three decades the humpback whale has become something of a wildlife celebrity. It is one of the most widely recognized large whales, and its acrobatic displays, inquisitive personality, and intricate and varied songs have earned it a place in the affections of humans.

But the story has not always been a positive one. Prior to the worldwide ban on whaling in the mid-1980s the humpback had been one of the most widely hunted species and came within a whisker of extinction. A relatively slow-swimming animal, the humpback made an easy target, especially when large herds gathered in shallow coastal waters to breed. They were easy to approach, often coming close to whaling boats out of curiosity and discovering the danger too late. Commercial hunting of humpbacks dates back over 300 years, and before that many aboriginal peoples killed humpbacks for subsistence using simple hand-made weapons. These traditional hunts are still permitted, but the quotas are very low and are reviewed from year to year.

A Booming Industry

The ban on whaling has been so successful that by 2010 the world population of humpbacks was believed to have returned to the level of 1940. Many former whaling communities have developed into ecotourism resorts specializing in whalewatching. The profits from this rapidly expanding industry have reduced the pressure to resume hunting and played a significant part in the species' recovery. Nevertheless, it is important that the whales are not disturbed by excessive pressure from boatloads of excited tourists.

Humpback Behavior

Humpbacks are among the most vocal of whales and their long, complex songs, hauntingly beautiful to the human ear, feature in popular music, classical compositions, and relaxation therapies. The songs, which last anything up to half an hour, vary slightly from place to place—a bit like human dialects—and they change gradually over time as whales pick up variations from each other. Like birdsong, these sounds are generally used by solitary males and are thought to attract females and let other whales know who is around.

Other fascinating aspects of humpback behavior include their feeding techniques. They generally filter feed in a similar manner to other baleen whales, but have also developed some rather special techniques of their own. One of the most impressive is bubble-netting, whereby one or more whales swims in an upward spiral around a shoal of fish, releasing a steady stream of bubbles that form a dense curtain through which the fish will not swim. The fish bunch closer together and move upward to escape the circling whales; but once they reach the surface, they are trapped, and the whales move in, swallowing huge mouthfuls of fish and water. The furrows in the whale's throat allow it to expand so that it can gulp in hundreds of densely shoaling fish at a time.

The nets used by fishing crews are curtains of death for whales as well as fish. Once entangled in the mesh, a humpback is usually doomed. Along with disturbance from boats, these nets are one of the major threats to humpback whales today.

The humpback whale *is one of the most popular species for whale-watchers; it is large, curious about boats, and often apparently full of high spirits. For an ever-increasing number of people an encounter with whales is the highlight of a vacation if not the experience of a lifetime.*

DATA PANEL

Humpback whale (humpwhale, hunchbacked whale)

Megaptera novaeangliae

Family: Balaenopteridae

World population: More than 30,000

Distribution: Global

Habitat: Mostly deep ocean but ventures into shallower waters to breed

Size: Length head/body: 36–46 ft (11–14 m); occasionally up to 50 ft (15 m); female slightly larger than male. Weight: 33 tons (30 tonnes)

Form: Large dark-gray to black baleen whale with tapering, knobby head; pectoral fins very long (one-third body length) and patterned with irregular and unique white markings; tail flukes (lobes) also large and often marked with white

Diet: Small shoaling fish and crustaceans

Breeding: Single young born in tropics during temperate winter after 11-month gestation, usually every other year; weaned at 11 months; mature at 4–6 years. May live up to 77 years

Related endangered species: Blue whale *(Balaenoptera musculus)* EN; fin whale *(B. physalus)* EN; sei whale *(B. borealis)* EN; minke whale *(B. acutorostrata)* LRnt

Status: IUCN LC

Proboscis Monkey

Nasalis larvatus

The proboscis monkey was once fortunate enough to live in one of the world's most inaccessible and undisturbed areas. Today, despite government protection, the species is endangered because of destruction of its mangrove forest habitat.

Until quite recently the extraordinary-looking proboscis monkey was relatively common on its native island of Borneo. Even while other native primates—such as the orang-utan—were suffering dramatic population declines, the proboscis monkey appeared to be holding its own. The main reason for its success was its inaccessible habitat; the species lives in some of the most impenetrable places on the island, namely, the dense mangrove forests that once lined many of the region's rivers. Mangroves form a dense mass of branches and stems, standing in water and soft mud. It is virtually impossible to walk around in mangrove thickets, which may extend unbroken for many miles. Animals living there are fairly safe and have adapted to climb and scramble around with ease. While the stable rain forest of Borneo's interior was being felled for timber and wood pulp, or cleared for agriculture, the mangroves remained inaccessible to machinery, and the space they occupied was unsuitable for agriculture. The waterlogged forest had little commercial value and was left to the proboscis monkeys and other specialized mangrove wildlife.

A Life Near Water

Proboscis monkeys are the most aquatic of all the primates. Their partially webbed feet make them excellent swimmers, and they sometimes use the water as a convenient emergency escape route. Alarmed monkeys will readily plunge 50 feet (15 m) from a treetop to the relative safety of the water. Such a jump onto dry land would result in serious injury, even for an agile primate.

The monkeys tend not to feed in the water, surviving instead on a diet of leaves plucked from the trees. The leaves are generally tough and not nutritious, so they have to be eaten in large quantities. It has been estimated that the contents of an adult proboscis monkey's stomach accounts for about a quarter of its body weight. The huge meals pass slowly through the monkey's digestive system and are broken down by special gut-dwelling bacteria. The bacteria also break down some of the toxic chemicals produced by mangroves and many other forest plants,

DATA PANEL

Proboscis monkey

Nasalis larvatus

Family: Cercopithecidae

World population: Unknown but decreasing

Distribution: Borneo

Habitat: Freshwater mangrove and lowland rain forest

Size: Length head/body: 21–30 in (53–76 cm); tail: 22–30 in (56–76 cm); males twice as big as females. Weight: 17–30 lb (7–22 kg)

Form: Large, long-tailed monkey with variable red-brown fur that fades to white on underside. Feet partially webbed. Nose is small and snub in juveniles and females; large and pendulous in males

Diet: Mostly leaves of pedada trees; some fruit seeds; also flowers

Breeding: Single young born at any time of year after 24-week gestation. Life span unknown; probably at least 10 years .

Related endangered species: No close relatives, but at least 35 other species of Old World monkey family Cercopithecidae are classified as Vulnerable or Endangered

Status: IUCN EN

enabling the proboscis monkey to take advantage of food that other animals have to avoid.

A Nose for Success

The large nose of the mature male proboscis monkey is what gives the species its name, but its precise purpose is unknown. Being much larger than females, males are more prone to overheating: One theory is that the nose acts as a cooling device, radiating excess body heat. It may also be that the large nose is a badge of success, since it continues to grow throughout a male's life; the males with the largest noses are the oldest and presumably, therefore, the fittest and most successful breeders. In choosing a suitable male to father her offspring, a female may use the size of a male's nose as an indicator of his genetic desirability.

Reduced Circumstances

It would be a tragedy if proboscis monkey numbers were reduced by so much that the species became more famous for being rare than for its other unique characteristics. However, its future is uncertain. The mangroves that provide its home are now harvested for wood, and modern drainage technology has meant that the watery world of the proboscis monkey is being invaded by developers. The rivers that once flooded the forests—creating natural refuges for wildlife—have been tamed, and in just a few decades well over half of Borneo's mangrove forest has disappeared. Previously extensive mangrove swamps have been reduced to narrow fringes along rivers and no longer supply adequate habitat for the monkeys.

There are a few proboscis monkeys in captivity. However, the species is considered difficult to keep in zoos, perhaps because it is not easy to re-create its natural mangrove habitat in artificial conditions. With the entire wild population confined to one island, the priority must be the preservation of its habitat.

The male proboscis monkey's *extraordinary nose makes it one of the most easily recognized of all primates. Females and youngsters have small, upturned noses.*

Chimpanzee

Pan troglodytes

Despite its protected status, a shrinking habitat and continued poaching are major problems facing Africa's "common" chimpanzee, and populations are rapidly dying out.

Throughout central Africa human populations are expanding, and there is a growing pressure on the land from people trying to make a living. In many areas everyday human practices are putting chimpanzees at risk. Despite the fact that this animal is a close relative—we share 98 percent of our genes with chimps—it receives little sympathy when it becomes a competitor for space.

Although wild chimpanzees are protected by law in several African countries, regulations are difficult to enforce, especially in areas of central Africa torn apart by political instability and civil war. Moreover, legal protection does not include protection of their habitat.

The tropical forests, already reduced to a fraction of their original size, continue to be logged and cleared for agriculture. The remaining areas are often so disturbed by people hunting, collecting firewood, or herding their livestock that the chimpanzee population moves on or dies out. Today wild chimpanzees live in isolated patches of habitat, some of which are too small to support a healthy, viable population. As a result, levels of inbreeding increase, leading to genetic problems and birth defects.

Nevertheless, in some areas the chimpanzees are traditionally tolerated and respected, even to the extent that they are allowed to wander into crop fields and village markets. Local people do no more than "shoo" them away if they become a nuisance.

Chimpanzees *are stocky, powerful animals that use a combination of brainpower and brawn to survive in a variety of habitats, including rain forests, deciduous forests, and swamp forests. They are even capable of making and using tools.*

DATA PANEL

Chimpanzee (common chimpanzee)

Pan troglodytes

Family: Pongidae

World population: 172,700–299,700

Distribution: Tropical western and central Africa, from Senegal and Angola to Tanzania and Sudan

Habitat: Rain forest, deciduous forest, swamp forest, and savanna grassland with access to evergreen fruiting trees

Size: Length: 28–38 in (71–97 cm); height at shoulder: 39–66 in (95–165 cm); males slightly larger than females. Weight: 66–110 lb (30–50 kg)

Form: Large ape covered in long, brown-black hair. Palms and face are bare; adults are sometimes bald. Skin on face is wrinkled, usually pink or brown, darkening with age. Projecting jaw has large, expressive lips

Diet: Fruit, leaves; also seeds, shoots, bark, flowers, honey, and insects; some meat from smaller animals, including monkeys and wild pigs

Breeding: Single young born at any time of year after gestation of 7–8 months; weaned at 3–4 years; stays with mother until mature at 7 years. Life span may exceed 35 years

Related endangered species: western lowland gorilla (*Gorilla gorilla gorilla*) CR; mountain gorilla (*Gorilla gorilla beringei*) EN; Bornean orang-utan (*Pongo pygmaeus*) EN; pygmy chimpanzee (*Pan paniscus*) EN

Status: IUCN EN

However, this kind of tolerance is the exception to the rule: In other parts of their range chimpanzees are treated as pests and killed to protect crops. Some are caught in snares or shot and eaten as bush meat. Their body parts have also been used in traditional medicines and rituals. Perhaps most disturbing of all, chimpanzees are captured live and sold as pets or for medical research. This trade represents a huge loss of life; for every young chimp that reaches its final destination, several more will have died in transit. The young chimps' mothers are often also killed in the poachers' efforts to kidnap the baby.

A Captive Future

There are large numbers of chimpanzees in captivity all around the world. Many are kept as illegal pets or held in unlicensed collections, but a great number are in zoos and conservation centers. Of those born and bred in captivity, some are of mixed race, with parents from different regions of Africa who would never normally have met in the wild. It is unlikely that any of these captive-raised chimpanzees will be successfully returned to the wild. Like human babies, young chimpanzees are born with few

instincts and must learn from their elders the skills they need to survive. Individuals born in captivity have often been hand-reared by keepers and are therefore ill-equipped for life in the wild. They are also likely to have difficulty in rearing their own young. In addition, captive chimpanzees may carry diseases that could destroy a wild population.

There is more hope for wild-born chimpanzees that have been rescued from illegal collections. Animals such as these can be taken to one of several rehabilitation centers in Africa where they can practice their "wild" skills in large enclosures before being set free. However, releases are still risky. The danger of disease, or of chimpanzees being attacked by established populations, means that they are usually released in areas from which the species has already disappeared.

Mountain Gorilla

Gorilla gorilla beringei

After years of intensive conservation efforts Africa's mountain gorilla population seemed to be overcoming the threat of extinction. However, civil war in the region has since undone much of the progress that had been made.

Mountain gorillas are particularly vulnerable to environmental pressures, both natural and human-made, because of their slow breeding rate, which makes it difficult for them to replenish their numbers. Usually only one baby is born at a time; but on the rare occasions when twins occur, one almost always dies.

Most female gorillas do not breed until they are at least 10. A female can bear young every four years; but because many infants die before they are two, the rate for successful reproduction is closer to one every eight years. Even a female living in exceptionally favorable conditions is unlikely to rear more than six offspring in her 40-year lifetime. It is more likely that she will raise between two and four young. The young are not fully weaned until the age of three and remain with their mothers for several more years.

Major Threats

The major problems facing the mountain gorilla in the mid-20th century were poaching, kidnapping, and habitat loss. Such problems can be prevented by setting aside areas of gorilla habitat and patrolling them to prevent hunting. Such refuges did exist, but the protection provided in the past was nowhere near adequate. Many hundreds were still illegally caught in snares, their flesh sold as bush meat, and their heads, hands, and feet made into trophies and tourist souvenirs. There was also a thriving market in live baby gorillas, a trade made all the more abhorrent by the fact that poachers usually killed the mother, or the entire family, to kidnap one baby. Mountain gorillas do not cope well with captivity—those seen in zoos are of

the lowland variety—and few kidnapped youngsters survive. Huge areas of mountain gorilla habitat were lost to cultivation in the 1950s and 1960s. The matter came to a head in 1968 when a single refuge, representing 40 percent of the gorillas' remaining habitat, was turned over to agriculture.

Changing Fortunes

By the late 1960s it was clear that if mountain gorillas were to escape extinction, both the animals and their shrinking habitat needed proper protection. For two decades this was provided, and at the end of the 1980s the mountain gorilla's prospects were looking much brighter. The Rwandan gorilla population had increased by over 20 percent; special reserves gave them a secure habitat, and an intensive education program helped local people realize the value of their great ape neighbors. The gorillas became a national treasure and the focus of a lucrative ecotourism industry, which in 1990 ranked as Rwanda's third highest source of income. Similar projects were also reaping benefits in neighboring Uganda and the Democratic Republic of Congo (formerly Zaire). Ecotourism brings in money, and the presence of visitors makes it more difficult for poachers to operate unseen, but the visitors also bring disease. Gorillas are susceptible to human infections, and there is a risk of passing on flu viruses and other germs to the animals when tourists visit the forests.

Civil wars and the refugee crises that result from them have put huge pressure on the land in Rwanda and the Democratic Republic of Congo. In 2007, at least eight gorillas were shot dead in three incidents in

DATA PANEL

Mountain gorilla

Gorilla gorilla beringei

Family: Pongidae

World population: 680

Distribution: Mountains linking the Democratic Republic of Congo, Rwanda, and Uganda, eastern Africa

Habitat: Cloud forests on volcanic slopes at 5,450–12,500 ft (1,650–3,800 m)

Size: Height: 5–9 ft (1.5–1.8 m); male up to twice the size of female. Weight: 154–440 lb (70–200 kg)

Form: Large, powerful ape. Dark brown-black hair, longer than that of lowland gorilla. Walks on all fours using soles of feet and knuckles of hands; arms shorter than those of lowland gorilla. Dominant males very large with silvery hair on back

Diet: Leaves, roots, and shoots; some bark, flowers, fruit, fungi; occasionally invertebrates and even dung

Breeding: Single young born at any time of year after 8-month gestation; births at intervals of at least 4 years; young weaned at 3 years; mature at 10 years (female) or 15 years (male). Life span up to 40 years in wild

Related endangered species: Western lowland gorilla *(Gorilla gorilla gorilla)* CR; eastern lowland gorilla *(G. g. graueri)* EN; chimpanzee *(Pan troglodytes)* EN; pygmy chimpanzee *(P. paniscus)* EN; Bornean orang-utan *(Pongo pygmaeus)* EN

Status: IUCN EN

Virunga National Park, D. R. Congo. These losses amount to about 3 percent of the Virunga population of gorillas. Rebel control of part of the area in 2008–2009 made it impossible for the park authorities to monitor the gorillas' numbers. It seems there may not be enough room to accommodate both the gorillas and the thousands of people in need of land.

The mountain gorilla
is the world's largest primate, but despite its huge size and obvious strength, it is also one of the gentlest.

Orang-Utan

Pongo pygmaeus

Orang-utan means "man of the forest" in the Malay language. Once numbering hundreds of thousands, the orang-utan population has declined sharply in recent years because of loss of habitat and capture for the pet trade.

The orang-utan holds two animal records: It is the world's largest tree-dwelling mammal, and it is the only great ape that lives in Asia. Living in the trees of the tropical rain forests of Borneo and Sumatra, this ape rarely walks on the ground. It has very long, strong arms ideally suited to a life of swinging and climbing from branch to branch in the tree canopy.

Orang-utans tend to live alone or in very small groups. Most nights they build a fresh nest in the trees, only occasionally reusing a nest. Two-thirds of their diet is fruit—especially wild figs and durians —but they have a huge appetite and may spend a whole day sitting gorging in a tree.

Orang-utans can live for up to 40 years; they are mature aged between seven and 10. Females normally give birth to a single baby, though occasionally they have twins. The babies are completely dependent on the mother and are not weaned until three years old.

Decline and Fall

Once orang-utans were found throughout Southeast Asia and southern China, but there are now estimated to be fewer than 70,000 in the wild and the figure may be much smaller. Their numbers declined by 30 to 50 percent in the last 10 years of the 20th century.

The greatest threat to orang-utans is the destruction of their habitat—tropical rain forest. Large areas of forest have been affected as trees are felled for their timber, and land cleared for farming. It is estimated that 80 percent of all forest in Malaysia and Indonesia has already been logged. In the 1990s a series of forest fires that burned for months at a time badly affected the orang-utan.

Another threat is the capture of live orang-utans for the pet trade. Despite legislation, in early 2004 about 100 Bornean orang-utans were confiscated in Thailand; 50 of them were sent back to Borneo two years later. For every orang-utan that survives capture and shipment, five or six others will die in the process.

The highly intelligent species is protected by law in Indonesia and Malaysia; both countries have signed up

DATA PANEL

Orang-utan

Pongo pygmaeus

Family: Pongidae

World population: 45,000–69,000, declining

Distribution: Indonesia (Kalimantan, Sumatra) and Malaysia (Sabah, Sarawak)

Habitat: Tropical rain forests

Size: Height: male 54 in (137 cm); female 45 in (115 cm). Weight: male 130–200 lb (60–90 kg); female 88–110 lb (40–50 kg)

Form: A large long-haired ape; the coat is usually a reddish color but varies from orange to dark chocolate

Diet: Mainly fruit; also young leaves and shoots, insects, bark, and small mammals

Breeding: Usually gives birth to single young; mature at 7–10 years. Life span up to 40 years

Related endangered species: Western lowland gorilla (*Gorilla gorilla gorilla*) CR; mountain gorilla (*G. g. beringei*) EN; pygmy chimpanzee (*Pan paniscus*) EN; chimpanzee (*P. troglodytes*) EN

Status: IUCN EN

to CITES. The 1987 Asian Primate Action Plan identified several conservation measures needed to protect the orang-utan. They included the setting up and managing of protected areas (such as the Gunung National Park in Sumatra), surveys to establish the population and distribution of orang-utans, and a public education program. About 60 percent of orang-utans in Borneo could be protected if conservation laws were more rigorously enforced.

There are a number of orang-utan rehabilitation centers. They look after orang-utans rescued from smugglers or those that have lost their homes because of logging. The apes are relocated to protected areas. Several hundred orang-utans are held in zoos and collections worldwide—many of which were born in captivity.

Orang-utans *are fascinating apes that share 96.4 percent of the genes that make up the human genetic code.*

Ruffed Lemur

Varecia variegata

The ruffed lemur is the largest of the true lemurs and is becoming so rare in the wild that its best hope for survival is now an intensive program of captive breeding and release.

The ruffed lemur of Madagascar stands out among other lemurs because of its large size and distinctively patterned coat. The patterns and colors vary, but fall into two main subspecies: the red ruffed lemur and the black-and-white ruffed lemur. By far the most endangered is the red ruffed lemur, which only occurs in the far north of the species' range. Trapping and shooting are widespread activities in the area, and the local forest is being destroyed at such a rate that the IUCN predicts that unless effective action is taken, the population will plummet by at least half in the next few years.

The prospects for the black-and-white ruffed lemur are slightly brighter, although it is still a highly endangered animal. Its range is much larger than that of the red ruffed lemur, but the population is sparsely distributed. The black-and-white ruffed lemur occurs in several nature reserves, including the small island of Nosy Mangabe, where the species was introduced in the 1930s. Here the population density is much higher than elsewhere—over 30 animals per square mile (19 per sq. km). Even at these densities there are probably no more than 150 animals in total, and the population is regularly raided by poachers.

Captive Breeding

The ruffed lemur has shown that it will take very easily to captivity, but its adaptability has been a mixed blessing. On the one hand, collecting for the Malagasy pet trade has played a large part in the species' decline. On the other, it means that there are large numbers living in the safety of zoos and conservation institutions around the world. Of the captive population, about 500 are black-and-white ruffed and 300 are red ruffed lemurs.

Over 95 percent of the population in zoos and other institutions are captive born, and there is now an extensive international breeding program, coordinated by San Diego Zoo. One problem with captive breeding is keeping the gene pool as large as possible. Although interbreeding between subspecies is strongly discouraged, there are a small number of hybrids in existence. Zoos cooperate by lending out animals for breeding so that the captive populations remain as genetically diverse as possible.

A few ruffed lemurs were successfully released back into the wild in 1998 and 1999, and at least one captive-

DATA PANEL

Ruffed lemur (variegated lemur)

Varecia variegata

Family: Lemuridae

World population: Unknown, but probably fewer than 10,000

Distribution: Eastern Madagascar

Habitat: Rain forest from sea level to 3,900 ft (1,200 m)

Size: Length head/body: 20–24 in (51–60 cm); tail: 22–25 in (56–65 cm); females larger than males. Weight: 7–10 lb (3.2–4.5 kg)

Form: Large lemur with thick, variable coat. Black-and-white and red forms both have a white ruff, or neck patch

Diet: Fruit, leaves, seeds, and nectar; occasionally earth

Breeding: Between 2 and 6 young born after gestation of 3–3.5 months; weaned at 19 weeks; mature at 20 months; breeds before 36 months

Related endangered species: Golden bamboo lemur *(Hapalemur aureus)* EN; greater bamboo lemur *(Prolemur simus)* EN; 5 other members of the Lemuridae family are classified as Vulnerable

Status: IUCN CR

COMOROS

MADAGASCAR

MOZAMBIQUE

The ruffed lemur *has two distinct subspecies, the red ruffed (main picture) and black-and-white ruffed (inset). Some zoologists believe they should be treated as separate species. Even within the two subgroups the coat patterns are extremely variable, leading some experts to recommend that they are further divided into seven subspecies.*

born female has raised a family since being released back into the wild. In years to come it is hoped that the captive-bred individuals will become the founders of stable new populations in specially protected areas of the species' former range.

Conservation Policies and Problems

Before the successful reintroduction of captive-bred lemurs can take place there needs to be a significant improvement in the way that Malagasy conservation law is enforced. Although conservation policies are in place, it is not easy for the government to make a real commitment to them in a country where the population is so poor, and where many other social and economic issues take priority. There have been instances, for example, where Malagasy nature reserves have been given up in favor of commercial logging. In addition, poaching has been allowed to continue virtually unchecked in areas that are supposedly protected.

The relatively recent development of ecotourism on Madagascar is now bringing money and trade to the island, showing both the government and local people that conservation can pay. A real change of attitude toward conservation of the island's wildlife by the local population would give the ruffed lemur a fighting chance of survival.

African Elephant

Loxodonta africana

The African elephant is the largest land mammal on earth. It is a remarkable creature, not only because of its size and bulk, but also because of its intelligence, memory, and behavior.

The statistics surrounding the African elephant are as impressive as the animal itself: It is the world's largest land mammal and has the longest gestation of any animal (660 days—nearly two years). An adult elephant can drink between 15 and 20 gallons (70 and 90 l) of water a day and eat about 330 pounds (150 kg) of food. Despite its size and weight, however, an African elephant can reach speeds of 25 miles per hour (40 km/h) when charging or fleeing.

The elephant's distinctive trunk has many functions. It is used for feeding, carrying, spraying water or dust to cool itself, making sounds, greeting other elephants, threatening, stroking, and even as a pacifier for baby elephants to suck on. Elephants have long tusks made of ivory that they use for fighting and digging; they flap their large ears to keep cool in the African heat.

The Romans wrote about elephants living on the Mediterranean coast of North Africa, but today African elephants can only be found on the savanna grasslands and forests south of the Sahara Desert. There they feed on the grasses and foliage, sometimes ripping trees out with their trunks and stripping them of bark and leaves. The female elephants (cows) live in herds with their calves and close female relatives. The herd is led by the oldest female elephant, called the matriarch. Male elephants (bulls) leave the herd when they reach puberty. They live alone or in small bachelor groups, only joining a herd again to mate.

Elephants live for about 70 years. They are social animals and have been known to work together—particularly in times of danger—to help sick or injured family members. They are also thought to grieve for their dead relatives.

DATA PANEL

African elephant

Loxodonta africana

Family: Elephantidae

World population: 470,000–690,000

Distribution: Sub-Saharan Africa

Habitat: Savanna grasslands; forests

Size: Length: up to 16.4 ft (5 m); height at shoulder: up to 10.8 ft (3.3 m); males 10% bigger than females. Weight: male up to 6.7 tons (6 tonnes); female up to 3.3 tons (2.9 tonnes)

Form: Huge gray-black body with columnlike legs, large head, large ears, long tusks, and a flexible trunk; little hair on skin

Diet: Grasses, tree leaves, and bark

Breeding: Breeds at 13 or 14 years old; gestation of nearly 2 years. Calves every 3–4 years in wet season. May live up to 70 years

Related endangered species: Asian elephant *(Elephas maximus)* EN

Status: IUCN VU

African elephants flap their large ears to keep themselves cool. This elephant is red from dust bathing—another way of cooling off.

African elephant populations fell dramatically during the 20th century. At the start of the century there were many millions, in 1970 there were 2 million, and by 2000 there were probably fewer than half a million. However, this trend has since been reversed (see figures in data panel).

Trade and Land

Ivory from elephant tusks is a prized material traditionally used to make carvings and jewelry. The trade in ivory began seriously in the 17th century, when Arab traders hunted elephants in West Africa. The invention of guns, and in particular the rifle, meant that hunters could kill animals more efficiently. African elephants are now protected in many countries, and there is an official ban on trade in ivory.

However, there is still a strong demand for the tusks, and illegal poaching is widespread.

Elephants are also threatened by loss of habitat. As the growing human population of Africa demands more land for expanding cities and for farmland, the elephants' habitat has shrunk, limiting their access to food. This can bring them into conflict with humans, since elephants may be driven by hunger to raid crops.

After pressure by conservation organizations the African elephant was put on Appendix I of CITES in 1989, banning international trade in the species and its products. However, several African countries want to continue trading to earn money for conservation.

Conservation groups run projects in Africa strengthening elephant conservation through anti-poaching patrols, education, and trade controls. They also work with local people to reduce conflict between elephants and humans and to promote the benefits of elephants to the local tourist industry.

Black Rhinoceros

Diceros bicornis

Formerly abundant and widespread in Africa, the black rhinoceros has been drastically reduced in numbers since the 1970s. The main culprit is the expanding international trade in rhino horn.

Although the black rhinoceros is able, if necessary, to go for five days without water, it is generally found in relatively moist areas of lush vegetation. Throughout Africa these regions are under pressure for development into farm and grazing land, effectively excluding the rhinos, which are too large and unpredictable to be tolerated close to human settlements. Yet the main threat to the animals comes not so much from habitat loss as from hunting, principally for their horns for use in oriental medicine.

For centuries rhino horn, composed of densely compressed hair, has been powdered and swallowed as a remedy for fevers and other disorders. It is made of keratin (a fibrous substance that occurs in skin, hair, nails, and hooves) and cannot be absorbed into the body, so any supposed medicinal benefits will only be imaginary. Yet the horns continue to fetch high prices, often earning more than their weight in gold.

In recent years a new factor has further complicated the situation. In Yemen in southwestern Asia there has long been a tradition of using rhino horn to make carved dagger handles. As oil money brought new prosperity to the region, the demand for these prestigious status symbols increased; in 1999 more than 100 craftsmen were employed in making and repairing such artifacts. Old and new horns were used; at the time, new horns were said to be fetching $615 per pound ($1,350 per kg), 20 percent more than they had only two years earlier.

Before hunting reduced their numbers, black rhinos could be found in the bush and savanna regions of most of Africa south of the Sahara. By the 1960s they were already becoming rare, but were still widely distributed, with substantial numbers in Kenya,

Tanzania, and Zimbabwe. Although the animals enjoyed legal protection, the lucrative trade in horns could not be controlled, and the rhino died out in one area after another as hunting took its lethal toll.

Slow Breeders

The black rhino has one of the slowest reproductive rates of any large mammal, making it ill-equipped to cope with population loss. Young animals first breed at five or even 10 years, but in practice many are killed long before they reach that age. Calves are not born annually, but at intervals of up to five years. In the past this was not a disadvantage; the slow breeding rate was probably a natural adaptation to avoid producing more young than the available resources could support. Excessive hunting has, however, overwhelmed the animal's capacity to maintain its numbers, which have fallen by more than 90 percent since 1970. The total figure now seems to have stabilized, but several countries where the species was

Black rhinos *are usually tolerant of each other, but can be aggressive toward humans. Their temperamental behavior makes them difficult to manage; incidents involving rogue animals do not help the species' cause.*

once common now have fewer than 50 black rhinos, most of them confined to national parks and reserves.

Thanks to the high cash value of the horns, the killing continues; a poacher can earn more from one dead rhino than from a year's farmwork. One possible solution might be to remove the horns, which contain no nerve endings and can be painlessly cut away without disrupting the rhino's life. However, the horns grow back, so the process would have to be repeated. Even so, such a program would remove the incentive for poaching and might prove more practicable in the long run than captive breeding, which is the only other way of ensuring the rhino's long-term survival.

DATA PANEL

Black rhinoceros

Diceros bicornis

Family: Rhinocerotidae

World population: About 4,180 (2007 estimate)

Distribution: Africa south of the Sahara, in widely scattered localities

Habitat: Bush and savanna; rarely found more than a day's walk from water

Size: Length head/body: 9.5–12.3 ft (2.9–3.7 m); tail: 24–28 in (60–70 cm); height at shoulder: 4.5–5.9 ft (1.4–1.8 m). Weight: 1,500–3,000 lb (700–1,400 kg)

Form: Large, thick-skinned animal; grayish in color but often coated with dust or mud. Two horns on the snout and a pointed, mobile upper lip, used like a miniature trunk to gather food

Diet: Leaves, twigs, and branches browsed from more than 200 species of low-growing shrub

Breeding: Single calf born after 15-month gestation; suckled for up to 1 year. Life span may exceed 40 years

Related endangered species: White rhinoceros (*Ceratotherium simum*) NT; great Indian rhinoceros (*Rhinoceros unicornis*) VU; Javan rhinoceros (*R. sondaicus*) CR; Sumatran rhinoceros (*Dicerorhinus sumatrensis*) CR

Status: IUCN CR

Giant Otter Shrew

Potamogale velox

The giant otter shrew occupies a large range in Central Africa. Nevertheless, it is poorly known, and its future is blighted by hunting, deforestation, pollution, and general lawlessness in areas of political instability.

The three species of otter shrew living in Africa are the only mainland members of the tenrec family, which is otherwise found exclusively on the island of Madagascar. Tenrecs were among the first mammals to colonize Madagascar from mainland Africa. For many thousands of years they had the place to themselves, and they diversified into an extraordinary range of forms and habits.

However, the mainland cousins of these early mammalian pioneers did not have it quite so easy. With other kinds of mammals already occupying niches in Africa's diverse habitats, they had to find alternative specializations in order to survive. The mainland otter shrews have evolved so much and become so different to the Malagasy branch of the family that some zoologists place them in a separate family of their own. Two small species live in tiny areas of West Africa and Uganda, but the giant otter shrew occurs widely across Central Africa.

Coveted Creatures

The giant otter shrew is one of the world's largest aquatic insectivores, almost as big as a true otter. Its common name is an apt one, since its specialization to an aquatic lifestyle makes it look much like a small otter or mink. Like both otters and mink, the giant otter shrew has fine, dense fur. The hairs trap an insulating layer of air, giving the shrew a silvery appearance under the water and helping keep it warm—even in tropical Africa mountain streams can be chilly.

Unfortunately, the animal's splendid pelt is coveted by humans, and the giant otter shrew has been hunted for its skin in many parts of its range.

DATA PANEL

Giant otter shrew (giant African water shrew)

Potamogale velox

Family: Tenrecidae

World population: Unknown

Distribution: Central Africa, including Nigeria, Gabon, Cameroon, Central African Republic, Uganda, Kenya, Democratic Republic of Congo (formerly Zaire), Rwanda, Burundi, Tanzania, Zambia, and Angola

Habitat: Fast- and slow-moving streams from sea level to 5,900 ft (1,800 m)

Size: Length head/body: 11.5–14 in (29–35 cm); tail: 9.5–35 in (24.5–90 cm). Weight: 12–14 oz (340–400 g)

Form: Otterlike animal with cylindrical body, powerful tail, and short legs; fur short and dense, brown to black above, pale below; head has broad, flat snout with stiff whiskers, small eyes, and small ears

Diet: Freshwater crustaceans (mainly crabs); also mollusks, fish, insects, and amphibians

Breeding: Two litters of 1 or 2 young born at any time of year

Related endangered species: Pygmy otter shrew (*Micropotamogale lamottei*) EN; Ruwenzori otter shrew (*M. ruwenzorii*) NT; aquatic tenrec (*Limnogale mergulus*) VU

Status: IUCN LC

While hunting is to be discouraged, the decline in giant otter shrew numbers probably has more to do with habitat destruction than with direct killing. The animals live in streams that pass through forested areas. They do not venture far from the water, and it is possible that they could survive with only a narrow strip of trees on either side of the watercourse. It would certainly cost the timber companies little to leave such areas alone when they cut down the rest of the forest. However, such narrow corridors of habitat are less useful to the majority of nonaquatic, forest-dwelling mammals, and most conservationists would prefer to see much larger areas of forest being protected so that other animals could also benefit.

Habitat Erosion

One of the side effects of deforestation is a dramatic increase in soil erosion. Soil and silt—no longer bound up by tree roots or protected and enriched by a layer of humus—are washed into streams and rivers every time it rains. In the wet season especially, a clear stream becomes a torrent of muddy water, and the effect is not limited to deforested areas. The mud is carried miles downstream, contaminating habitat that would otherwise still be suitable for otter shrews.

The giant otter shrew *has many of the characteristics of a true otter, including a powerful tail for swimming. It also has a flattened snout, with the nose, eyes, and ears near the top of the head, allowing it to see, hear and breathe with only a fraction of its head above water.*

The shrews have poor sight at the best of times and tend to rely more on scent and touch to find their prey. With the help of their other senses they are able to trap prey in cloudy water, even if visibility is reduced to zero. However, otter shrews can only hunt successfully if there is plenty of prey around. With mud and silt blocking out the sunlight, few aquatic plants can grow, so plant-eating stream creatures are scarce. The gills and filter-feeding mechanisms of fish and crustaceans become clogged, and they soon die off, leaving the otter shrews with nothing to eat.

There are no otter shrews in captivity, and nobody knows how many survive in the wild. However, the rapid destruction of their habitat by local and upstream deforestation means that they are facing a serious decline, and the situation is worsening.

Mulgara

Dasycercus cristicauda

Mulgara numbers fluctuate widely throughout much of their range. Nevertheless, there is little doubt that in the 200 years since Europeans settled in Australia, the mulgara's range has shrunk and the population declined.

The status of the ratlike mulgara of central Australia is something of a mystery. It seems that local mulgara populations are prone to dramatic peaks and troughs, probably brought on by the unpredictable rains and droughts in their desert habitat. The mulgara population is more stable in some parts of its range than in others. It is considered common in the Northern Territories of central Australia, for example, while the few mulgara populations in neighboring Queensland fluctuate wildly; they are sometimes thought to be extinct, only to reappear at a later date.

To add to the confusion, it now seems that many of the animals formerly regarded as mulgaras may, in fact, be a different species, known as the ampurta. Ampurtas live in the east of the mulgara's range, and it is virtually impossible to tell the two types—be they species or subspecies—apart except by analysis of their DNA.

Shrinking Range

Mulgaras were once common over a wide area, including what are now the Northern Territories, South Australia, and Western Australia. There were also stable populations in Queensland and New South Wales. The only place they appear to be doing well now is the Northern Territories. Isolated populations survive in parts of Western Australia and also in a few sites on the borders of the Northern Territories with Queensland and South Australia.

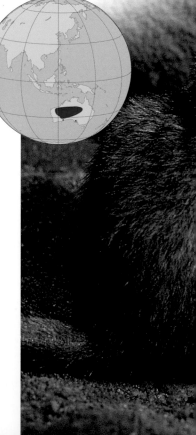

DATA PANEL

Mulgara (crest-tailed marsupial mouse)

Dasycercus cristicauda

Family: Dasyuridae

World population: Unknown; thought to fluctuate widely

Distribution: Widespread, but patchy in Western Australia, southern Northern Territories, and northern South Australia

Habitat: Sandy, semiarid grasslands

Size: Length: 5–8 in (12.5–22 cm); tail: 3–5 in (7–13 cm); males up to twice as large as females. Weight: 2–6 oz (60–170 g)

Form: Sandy-brown, ratlike marsupial; crest of black hairs blends into black fur on second half of tail; female lacks true pouch

Diet: Small mammals, reptiles, and invertebrates; seeds and root tubers

Breeding: Between 6 and 8 young born in May–June after 4-week gestation; remain attached to teat in fold of skin on belly for up to 2 months; independent at 4 months. Life span unknown

Related endangered species: Several other small species of insectivorous marsupial in Australia and New Guinea listed as VU or EN

Status: IUCN LC

The main causes of decline are predation by dingoes and introduced cats and dogs. The mulgara's habitat has also been altered and destroyed in places. The largest and best-known population is protected in the Uluru-Kata Tjita National Park in the Northern Territories, but even here not enough is known about the precise requirements of the mulgaras to ensure that the land is managed appropriately.

Picky Eaters

Mulgaras appear to be extremely fussy about their habitat. They live in burrows dug in dry, sandy soils and hunt for food among shoots of spinifex (a spiny-leaved inland grass also known as porcupine grass). However, mulgaras appear to prefer clumps that are about 10 years old, moving on when the centers of large old clumps begin to die off. They also avoid the new growth that springs up in the years after the grasses have been burned. Livestock farmers use regular controlled burning to keep down scrub and to encourage the growth of fresh new grass to feed their cattle and sheep. Cycles of natural burning and regrowth are a normal part of the mulgara's habitat; but when the farmers artificially set fire to the vegetation, the cycles are shorter. As a result, the spinifex rarely has long enough to develop and mature to the mulgaras' satisfaction.

The specific conditions favored by the mulgara are similar to those required by two other vulnerable Australian animals, the southern marsupial mole and the great desert skink (a type of lizard). Currently, conservationists are working on plans for controlling predators and maintaining suitable habitat that will benefit all three species.

The mulgara is small and ratlike in appearance. It feeds mainly on insects and small animals, and has many small, sharp teeth.

Kangaroo Island Dunnart

Sminthopsis aitkeni

Until survey work was carried out in 2000–2001, only a few Kangaroo Island dunnarts had ever been seen. It is both rare and elusive.

Until the late 1960s there were thought to be no dunnarts of any species living on Kangaroo Island off the coast of South Australia. However, in 1969 a domestic dog captured and killed two specimens of what appeared to be the common dunnart. It was reported that the dog had caught the mouselike animals as they fled from yacca trees that were being felled to make way for farmland. At the time common dunnarts were considered to be relatively abundant and widespread on the mainland of Australia. However, since they had never before been found on Kangaroo Island, the corpses were considered important enough to be sent to the Museum of South Australia in Adelaide. By the mid-1980s science had progressed sufficiently to allow closely related species to be distinguished by biochemical differences. As a result, many similar-looking animals could now be separated out and given the full species status they deserved. The common dunnart was a worthy candidate for such treatment. When specimens from different parts of Australia were processed in 1984, it became clear that there were, in fact, four species of "common dunnart" that had been grouped together because they looked so similar. Three of them—the common dunnart (from southeastern Australia), the little long-tailed dunnart, and Gilbert's dunnart (both from Western Australia)—appeared to be relatively secure. However, the newly named Kangaroo Island dunnart was an immediate conservation worry because no populations existed anywhere else.

Lack of Information

The Kangaroo Island dunnart appears to live in a variety of natural heathland habitats on the island; but the species is incredibly elusive, and its precise requirements are not known. The lack of sightings can be partly explained by the fact that the animals are

DATA PANEL

Kangaroo Island dunnart (sooty dunnart)

Sminthopsis aitkeni

Family: Dasyuridae

World population: Fewer than 500

Distribution: Kangaroo Island, South Australia

Habitat: Mallee (scrub) heathland

Size: Length head/body: 3–4 in (7.6–10 cm); tail: 3.5–4 in (9–10 cm); male about 10% larger than female. Weight: 0.7–0.9 oz (20–25 g)

Form: Mouselike marsupial with long, tapering snout and long tail; fur grayish tinged with sooty black on back

Diet: Probably insectivorous, like the closely related common dunnart

Breeding: Probably similar to common dunnart, with large litters born after short gestation; young weaned at about 2 months

Related endangered species: Boullanger Island gray-bellied dunnart (*Sminthopsis grisoventer*) LC; Julia Creek dunnart (*S. douglasi*) NT; sandhill dunnart (*S. psammophilla*) EN; Butler's dunnart (*S. butleri*) VU; Queensland common dunnart (*S. murina tatei*) LC

Status: IUCN CR

probably nocturnal. Like some of their mainland relatives, they may also go into a kind of hibernation during food shortages, seeking out secure refuges in which to hide. The absence of more detailed information is not due to a lack of effort. Indeed, there have been several attempts to survey the population using standard live-trapping techniques. So far all that biologists have learned is that the dunnart is rare—and cautious. After numerous trapping attempts only six individuals have been found, bringing the total of recorded specimens to just eight. What is almost certain is that wherever dunnarts live and breed on the island, they are at risk of dying out.

In 1983 laws were passed to protect native Australian vegetation, over 60 percent of which had already been cleared from Kangaroo Island for agriculture. Without knowing more about the dunnart's habitat, it is impossible to judge what effect land clearance might have had on numbers, or to take measures to safeguard its future.

Interim Measures

The manner in which the first Kangaroo Island dunnarts were discovered—they were caught by a domestic dog—showed only too clearly that introduced predators, including pets, are a serious threat to dunnart populations. The fact that such animals did not exist on Kangaroo Island until relatively recently may be the only reason the dunnarts have survived as long as they have. Until more is known about the species, the removal of predators and a complete ban on habitat disruption are the only measures that will have any chance of helping this endangered island mammal.

An extra-long tail *and black-tinted fur are the characteristics that set the Kangaroo Island dunnart apart from its common relative on the mainland. It was only recognized as a distinct species in 1984.*

Marsupial Mole

Notoryctes typhlops

Of all Australia's mammals, the marsupial moles of the western desert are certainly among the more unusual species. Since they normally spend almost their entire lives buried in the sandy soil, they are also among the least well understood.

Before declaring an animal Endangered, the IUCN normally needs convincing scientific evidence that the species is likely to become extinct unless the causes of the declining numbers are removed. In most cases the evidence for a species' decline is not difficult to come by—we can often easily see there are fewer individuals than there once were. Occasionally, however, there are exceptions; in the case of the marsupial moles of Australia the IUCN agreed to classify the species as Endangered even though most scientists who have tried to study the species admit that they have no idea how many marsupial moles there may be.

Marsupial moles are extraordinary for many reasons. In lifestyle and appearance they are very similar to African golden moles; but other than the fact that both are mammals, they are only distantly related. The similarities are a stunning example of what biologists call convergent evolution, where two completely different types of animal evolve into very similar forms because it is the best way of dealing with similar challenges of habitat or way of life. In the case of the marsupial mole the challenge is how to live buried in the desert sand.

Two of a Kind

The marsupial mole (sometimes also called the southern marsupial mole) has been known about since the 19th century. However, individuals are rarely seen—which is not surprising given the animal's way of life. In 1920 a new sort of marsupial mole was discovered close to Eighty Mile Beach on the northwestern coast of Western Australia. This variety, called the northern marsupial mole, was a little smaller than the southern marsupial mole, and it had a differently shaped nose-shield and tail.

Whether the northern marsupial mole qualifies as a separate species is the subject of a debate that is unlikely to be resolved, since the animals are so hard to find. However, from time to time specimens of the southern marsupial mole are discovered. People finding the moles are usually puzzled enough to contact a museum or university, and dead or dying specimens have been collected at a rate of five to 15 animals every 10 years.

The real challenge is to find and study a living marsupial mole of the northern variety. Scientists

---

DATA PANEL

Marsupial mole (southern marsupial mole)

Notoryctes typhlops

Family: Notoryctidae

World population: Unknown and almost impossible to estimate

Distribution: Northwestern Australia

Habitat: Desert burrows

Size: Length head/body: 4–6 in (10–16 cm); tail: 1 in (2.4 cm). Weight: 1.2–2.5 oz (35–70 g)

Form: Flat-bodied animal with pale-golden fur; very short legs; spadelike front feet; no functional eyes, ear hole hidden in fur; nose has tough, horny shield, tail short and stubby. Female has a pouch opening to rear

Diet: Insect grubs, particularly larvae of beetles and moths

Breeding: Unknown

Related endangered species: Northern marsupial mole (*Notoryctes caurinus*) DD

Status: IUCN DD

AUSTRALIA

have spent years searching the deserts, enlisting the support of local people living in remote Aboriginal communities. In 1998 two schoolboys found and captured a living specimen of the northern marsupial mole, which ended up at the Museum of Western Australia. It did not adapt to life in captivity and died after about eight weeks, having not eaten well in all that time.

Marsupial moles do occasionally come to the surface, usually after rain. When they emerge, their bodies leave distinctive furrows in the sand, with marks either side where they have used their legs to haul themselves along. Further proof that the moles are around can be found by taking core samples of firm sand and looking for the oval-shaped areas of looser material that show a mole has passed through. Scientists have tried burying sound-sensitive microphones in the sand to detect passing moles. The problem with all such techniques is that, while they show that there are moles around, they do not give any idea how many there are. Until researchers can get some idea about population size, it is very difficult to prove what position the species is in.

There is no shortage of goodwill toward the moles, since they do not appear to damage human activities such as farming. They have been killed out of curiosity or for their silky fur, but are not deliberately hunted. The marsupial moles' chief problem is likely to be changes in their habitat due to controlled burning of bush and grass to create grazing pastures. Predation by introduced species, such as cats, could be a problem too. A high proportion of fox droppings have been found to contain marsupial mole remains, thus proving that the marsupial mole's predators are better at finding them than people are.

The marsupial mole *has fine, sandy-colored silky fur and shovellike hands, which it uses to "swim" through sand. It can be found up to 5 feet (1.5 m) below the surface. It has no eyes or obvious ears, which would quickly clog with sand, and the female's pouch opens toward the rear, so it does not get full of sand.*

Koala

Phascolarctos cinereus

The koala has enjoyed considerable conservation success. However, although it is no longer threatened with extinction, managing the remaining populations is proving problematic for conservationists.

Koalas manage to survive on a diet that no other mammal will touch—eucalyptus leaves. Tough, dry, and with a very low nutritional value, the leaves also contain indigestible materials and compounds that are highly poisonous to most other animals. Koalas are able to exist on this poor diet by having efficient digestive systems that will not only break down the toxins but also extract every available calorie. They also conserve energy by spending up to 20 hours a day resting. Until the arrival of European settlers in Australia in the late 18th century the ability of the koala to eke out a living from a food that no other animal could eat meant that it was a highly successful animal, well adapted to its diet and environment.

Consequences of Colonization

European settlement brought a number of threats to Australia's native wildlife. It destroyed the natural habitat and caused a marked increase in forest fires. The koala was also hunted for its fur. By the early 20th century koalas were facing a very real threat of extinction. Disaster was narrowly averted when the koala was made a nationally protected species in 1927. The koala has now returned to much of its original range; but because its habitat is patchy, it will never be as common as it once was. Although the koala as a species is out of immediate danger, individuals and localized populations are still threatened. Many koalas are killed on the roads or attacked by dogs, and forest fires can wipe out whole colonies at a time.

Victims of Success

The biggest problem is the patchy, isolated nature of the remaining koala habitat. The species responds so well to conservation that protected populations often increase to the point where the animals begin to damage the trees that they rely on for survival. Yet surplus animals cannot easily disperse if their forest home is surrounded by urban development or vast areas of open pastureland, as is now the case in much of eastern Australia. In overcrowded

---

DATA PANEL

Koala

Phascolarctos cinereus

Family: Phascolarctidae

World population: Probably 80,000–100,000, but estimates vary widely and are controversial

Distribution: Eastern Australia

Habitat: Eucalyptus forests below 2,000 ft (600 m)

Size: Length head/body: 28–31 in (72–78 cm); animals from south of range larger than those in north. Weight: 11–24 lb (5–11 kg); males can be half as heavy again as females

Form: Stout, bearlike animal with thick, woolly, grayish-brown fur on back, fading to white on belly. Head large with rounded furry ears, beady black eyes, and large black nose. Legs short with 5 large claws on each foot.

Tail short and stumpy. Female has pouch that opens to the rear

Diet: Leaves of various species of eucalyptus

Breeding: Single young (occasionally twins) born in midsummer after gestation of 25–30 days; young spend 5–7 months in pouch, weaned at 6–12 months; mature at 2 years. Life span up to 20 years

Related endangered species: No close relatives, but the northern hairy-nosed wombat (*Lasiorhinus krefftii*) of northeastern Australia is listed as CR

Status: IUCN LC

AUSTRALIA

conditions the koala is especially vulnerable to a disease caused by the *Chlamydia psittaci* bacterium. Conservation programs therefore face the difficult task of establishing healthy koala populations without creating overpopulated, disease-ridden colonies in which surplus animals have to be culled.

The least damaging solution is to move the excess koalas to other areas of suitable habitat. However, after 200 years of logging, development, and clearance for agriculture there are very few large areas of eucalyptus forest available. Consequently, koalas are often moved to other isolated patches of woodland where they soon become overcrowded again. The only real solution is to create "corridors" of habitat linking the isolated patches so that koala populations can

Koalas, *like other Australian marsupials, are born very early and suckled by their mother—often in a pouch—for the first months of life. Koala young are weaned on to "pap," a special form of the mother's droppings that provides the baby with the gut bacteria it needs to digest eucalyptus leaves.*

spread themselves more evenly. Tracts of suitable land connecting isolated koala populations would benefit the species in other ways: When koala colonies are decimated by natural events such as forest fires or outbreaks of *Chlamydia*, koalas dispersing from other areas would be able to recolonize the affected sites.

Long-beaked Echidna

Zaglossus bruijnii

The long-beaked echidna is a reclusive animal that feeds mainly on the worms and small grubs it finds in the wet forest leaf litter. A slow breeder, it is hunted for food and suffers from habitat loss.

The long-beaked echidna is an egg-laying mammal that inhabits the thick, humid forests of New Guinea, an island north of Australia. It lives alone, sheltering in a burrow or other hideout during the day. Since it seems to be active largely at night and is rare, even in undisturbed habitats, it is difficult to study, and little is known of its habits. A 1998 report suggests that there may be three species of long-beaked echidna, but one is known from only a single specimen and may already be extinct.

Unlike its cousin the short-beaked echidna, which feeds extensively on ants and termites, the long-beaked echidna seems to specialize in eating worms. It seeks them out by poking its long, curved snout into rotting wood or under moss and leaves. The jaws do not open far, and they are weak and have no teeth, so the food must be swallowed without being chewed. Worms, beetle larvae, and grubs of all sorts are abundant in wet forest leaf litter, so there is normally sufficient food even for such a large creature.

Rare Animals

When the forests are cut down, the ground dries out, and the staple foods of the echidna's diet become less abundant. Felling trees also removes the availability of rotten wood, a vital source of invertebrate food. Large areas of forest have been cleared in New Guinea to make way for new villages, roads, mines, and farms. Still more has been felled for timber. The echidnas can now only survive in the remote areas where they are not troubled by such developments. They appear to have become extinct in the central highlands within the last 50 years, and they are no longer found in most of the northern areas of New Guinea.

Echidnas have been hunted by specially trained dogs and their meat is highly prized by native people as a rare delicacy to be eaten at traditional feasts. Echidnas cannot climb, run fast, or attack predators, so they are easily captured. It is said that echidnas live at an average density of 4 per square mile (1 or 2 per sq. km).

DATA PANEL

Long-beaked echidna

Zaglossus bruijnii

Family: Tachyglossidae

World population: Unknown, probably low thousands

Distribution: New Guinea (Papua New Guinea and West Irian, a province of Indonesia)

Habitat: Various habitats from lowland tropical jungles to mountain forests and grasslands at more than 13,000 ft (4,000 m) above sea level

Size: Length: 18–30 in (45–77 cm); height at shoulder: about 10 in (25 cm). Weight: 11–22 lb (5–10 kg)

Form: A small animal covered in short, thick spines and dense, black hair. Long, tubular, downcurved snout. Feet have large claws; hind ones point sideways; walks slowly with rolling gait

Diet: Invertebrates, mainly earthworms

Breeding: Details unknown, but probably lays 1 egg per year in July; egg is incubated in temporary pouch on the mother's belly. Young fed on milk for several months before becoming independent. A long-beaked echidna has lived more than 30 years in captivity; life span in the wild unknown

Related endangered species: Short-beaked echidna (*Tachyglossus aculeatus multiaculeatus*) LC

Status: IUCN CR

New Guinea

INDONESIA

PAPUA NEW GUINEA

AUSTRALIA

Multiplying this by the area of suitable habitat suggests that there may be over 300,000 animals in total, but such a figure is unlikely. In a sample of skulls from the remains of several thousand native animals killed for consumption in traditional feasts there was only one long-beaked echidna.

The long-beaked echidna breeds very slowly, producing only a single baby each year. The young are extremely vulnerable and almost defenseless for many months (apart from their spines). As a result of its slow breeding rate, the species is unable to sustain heavy losses. Echidnas are not at risk from large natural predators since there are none living on New Guinea. Consequently, their spines have evolved to offer the animal only limited protection. However, introduced dogs and increasing numbers of people present

The long-beaked echidna *is one of the few egg-laying mammals. In this young echidna (above) the black fur is not yet fully developed. The spines show up clearly in the photograph, taken at night with flash illumination.*

dangers that the animal cannot withstand. Long-beaked echidnas have full legal protection, but the law is not always enforced in remote areas.

Little is known about the breeding biology of echidnas; outside New Guinea specimens are kept in only one zoo in Sydney, Australia. Even the short-beaked echidna has rarely bred in captivity, so there seems to be little prospect of developing a "safety net" of captive-bred echidnas as an insurance against extinction. Maximum protection in the Lorenz National Park and other nature reserves in New Guinea is vital.

Platypus

Ornithorhynchus anatinus

Platypuses are no longer hunted for their fur, but they face threats from pollution and the environmental consequences of modern development. The platypus has become a well-known conservation symbol for its freshwater habitat of southeastern Australia.

European settlers in Australia first saw and described the duck-billed platypus in 1797, but it was another hundred years before the animal's unique anatomy and reproductive habits were scientifically studied. In the past the platypus was hunted extensively for its fur, which, like that of other aquatic mammals, is extremely dense, so it keeps the animal warm even when wet. Thousands of platypuses were killed for their skins, while the heads and bills were sold as curios.

Hunting has all but exterminated the platypus population of South Australia: The last sighting of the animals on the lower Murray River, one of Australia's major rivers, was as long ago as 1960. The only platypuses living in the state these days are an introduced population on Kangaroo Island off South Australia and a few animals in captivity. Today wild platypuses still occasionally come across the border from New South Wales.

People are not the only predators to have taken a serious toll. In the days before European settlement the only predator of the platypus was the native Australian water rat. In recent times, however, introduced foxes, cats, rats, and dogs have all killed platypuses, especially young ones. Road deaths are also becoming a problem in urban areas.

The Costs of Development

The main problems facing platypuses today are those associated with modern development. Pollution and physical changes threaten the waters where they live. Many rivers have become unsuitable for platypuses through dramatically altered rates of flow as a result of the diversion of water for human use. Artificial structures such as weirs, drains, dams, and grilles built

AUSTRALIA

DATA PANEL

Platypus (duck-billed platypus)

Ornithorhynchus anatinus

Family: Ornithorhynchidae

World population: Unknown; low thousands

Distribution: Fresh waters of eastern Australia; throughout Tasmania and King Island in the Bass Strait; introduced population on Kangaroo Island off South Australia

Habitat: Freshwater rivers, lakes, and lagoons

Size: Length: 12–22 in (30–55 cm); males up to 20% bigger than females on mainland, but in Tasmania the sexes are similarly sized. Weight: 1–5.5 lb (0.5–2.5 kg)

Form: Unlike any other mammal; body is robust and slightly flattened, covered in dense, brown fur; legs short, feet large and webbed; tail flattened from above and paddlelike; head dominated by large, soft, rubbery beak, eyes small, ears hidden in fur; male has prominent sharp spurs on hind feet

Diet: Mostly freshwater crustaceans, worms, and insect larvae; some small fish and frogs

Breeding: One to 3 (usually 2) sticky-shelled eggs laid August–October after 2-week gestation; incubated by mother for further 2 weeks before hatching; young feed on milk from ducts on mother's belly; weaned at 4–5 months; mature at 2 years. Life span up to 15 years in the wild

Related endangered species: No close relatives

Status: IUCN LC

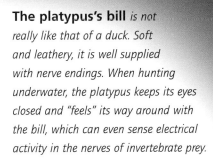

The platypus's bill *is not really like that of a duck. Soft and leathery, it is well supplied with nerve endings. When hunting underwater, the platypus keeps its eyes closed and "feels" its way around with the bill, which can even sense electrical activity in the nerves of invertebrate prey.*

across rivers to trap debris can make it difficult for platypuses to travel far.

Pollution is a problem for all freshwater animals. The particular threat for the platypus is that the fine, dense fur that it relies on for warmth underwater can be fouled by waste chemicals, while detergents in the water may destroy the natural oils that keep it waterproof. An adult platypus eats a great deal—up to half its own body weight every night—so anything that affects its food soon has a carry-over effect on platypus numbers. For example, nutrient enrichment by fertilizers washed off farmland may seem like the opposite of poisoning, but ultimately it is just as damaging. In a process known as "eutrophication" sudden blooms of algae—caused by the extra nutrients—can quickly choke a river or lake, using up all the available oxygen so that other plants and invertebrates cannot survive. It is also the case that some kinds of blue-green algae are highly toxic and can kill even quite large animals.

Studies of the platypus in captivity are allowing a better understanding of the problems it faces in the wild. For example, recent studies in South Australia—aimed at improving the success of captive-breeding programs—highlighted the importance of maintaining the natural chemical balance of the platypus's remaining wild habitat. Before 1990 only one platypus had ever been produced in captivity. As a result of the captive research it is now clear that factors such as the relative acidity of the water play a crucial role in breeding success.

The platypus is a popular animal that attracts much public attention. As such, it is a fine example of a "flagship species." Conservation measures designed to help it also benefit the rest of the ecosystem in which it lives. What is good for the platypus turns out to be helpful for less publicized aquatic creatures too.

Categories of Threat

The status categories that appear in the data panel for each species throughout this book are based on those published by the International Union for the Conservation of Nature (IUCN). They provide a useful guide to the current status of the species in the wild, and governments throughout the world use them when assessing conservation priorities and in policy-making. However, they do not provide automatic legal protection for the species.

Animals are placed in the appropriate category after scientific research. More species are being added all the time, and animals can be moved from one category to another as their circumstances change.

Extinct (EX)

A group of animals is classified as EX when there is no reasonable doubt that the last individual has died.

- Extinct (EX)
- Extinct in the Wild (EW)
- Critically Endangered (CR)
- Endangered (EN)
- Vulnerable (VU)
- Near Threatened (NT)
- Least Concern (LC)
- Data Deficient
- Not Evaluated

Adequate data

Threatened

Evaluated

Extinct in the Wild (EW)

Animals in this category are known to survive only in captivity or as a population established artificially by introduction somewhere well outside its former range. A species is categorized as EW when exhaustive surveys throughout the areas where it used to occur consistently fail to record a single individual. It is important that such searches be carried out over all of the available habitat and during a season or time of day when the animals should be present.

Critically Endangered (CR)

The category CR includes animals facing an extremely high risk of extinction in the wild in the immediate future. It includes any of the following:

- Any species with fewer than 50 individuals, even if the population is stable.
- Any species with fewer than 250 individuals if the population is declining, badly fragmented, or all in one vulnerable group.
- Animals from larger populations that have declined by 80 percent within 10 years (or are predicted to do so) or three generations, whichever is the longer.

The IUCN categories

of threat. The system displayed has operated for new and reviewed assessments since January 2001.

• Species living in a very small area—defined as under 39 square miles (100 sq. km).

Endangered (EN)

A species is EN when it is not CR but is nevertheless facing a very high risk of extinction in the wild in the near future. It includes any of the following:

• A species with fewer than 250 individuals remaining, even if the population is stable.

• Any species with fewer than 2,500 individuals if the population is declining, badly fragmented, or all in one vulnerable subpopulation.

• A species whose population is known or expected to decline by 50 percent within 10 years or three generations, whichever is the longer.

• A species whose range is under 1,900 square miles (5,000 sq. km), and whose range, numbers, or population levels are declining, fragmented, or fluctuating wildly.

• Species for which there is a more than 20 percent likelihood of extinction in the next 20 years or five generations, whichever is the longer.

Vulnerable (VU)

A species is VU when it is not CR or EN but is facing a high risk of extinction in the wild in the medium-term future. It includes any of the following:

• A species with fewer than 1,000 mature individuals remaining, even if the population is stable.

• Any species with fewer than 10,000 individuals if the population is declining, badly fragmented, or all in one vulnerable subpopulation.

• A species whose population is known, believed, or expected to decline by 20 percent within 10 years or

The orang-utan *is the largest arboreal (tree-dwelling) mammal on Earth. To thrive, the species requires large tracts of tropical forest and limited disturbance. Unfortunately, deforestation—for lumber or date palm cultivation—has reduced the area available to it. Despite conservation measures, orang-utan numbers continue to fall.*

three generations, whichever is the longer.
• A species whose range is less than 772 square miles (20,000 sq. km), and whose range, numbers, or population structure are declining, fragmented, or fluctuating wildly.
• Species for which there is a more than 10 percent likelihood of extinction in the next 100 years.

Near Threatened/Least Concern (since 2001)

In January 2001 the classification of lower-risk species was changed. Near Threatened (NT) and Least Concern (LC) were introduced as separate categories. They replaced the previous Lower Risk (LR) category with its subdivisions of Conservation Dependent (LRcd), Near Threatened (LRnt), and Least Concern (LRlc). From January 2001 all new assessments and reassessments must adopt NT or LC if relevant. But the older categories still apply to many animals until they are reassessed, and will also be found in this book.
• Near Threatened (NT)
Animals that do not qualify for CR, EN, or VU categories now but are close to qualifying or are likely to qualify for a threatened category in the future.
• Least Concern (LC)
Animals that have been evaluated and do not qualify for CR, EN, VU, or NT categories.

Lower Risk (before 2001)

• Conservation Dependent (LRcd)
Animals whose survival depends on an existing conservation program.
• Near Threatened (LRnt)
Animals for which there is no conservation program but that are close to qualifying for VU category.
• Least Concern (LRlc)

By monitoring *populations of threatened animals like this American rosy boa, biologists help keep the IUCN Red List up to date.*

CITES *regulations mean that elephant tusks can no longer be traded. The Kenyan government has destroyed its stockpiled ivory.*

Species that are not conservation dependent or near threatened.

Data Deficient (DD)

A species or population is DD when there is not enough information on abundance and distribution to assess the risk of extinction. In some cases, when the species is thought to live only in a small area, or a considerable period of time has passed since the species was last recorded, it may be placed in a threatened category as a precaution.

Not Evaluated (NE)

Such animals have not yet been assessed.

Note: a colored panel in each entry in this book indicates the current level of threat to the species. The two new categories (NT and LC) and two of the earlier Lower Risk categories (LRcd and LRnt) are included within the band LR; the old LRlc is included along with Data Deficient (DD) and Not Evaluated (NE) under "Other," abbreviated to "O."

CITES *lists animals in the major groups in three Appendices, depending on the level of threat posed by international trade.*

	Appendix I	Appendix II	Appendix III
Mammals	277 species 16 subspecies 14 populations	295 species 12 subspecies 12 populations	45 species 8 subspecies
Birds	152 species 11 subspecies 2 populations	1,268 species 6 subspecies 1 populations	35 species
Reptiles	75 species 5 subspecies 6 populations	527 species 4 subspecies 4 populations	55 species
Amphibians	16 species	98 species	
Fish	15 species	71 species	
Invertebrates	62 species 4 subspecies	2,100 species 1 subspecies	17 species

CITES APPENDICES

Appendix I lists the most endangered of traded species, namely those that are threatened with extinction and will be harmed by continued trade. These species are usually protected in their native countries and can only be imported or exported with a special permit. Permits are required to cover the whole transaction—both exporter and importer must prove that there is a compelling scientific justification for moving the animal from one country to another. This includes transferring animals between zoos for breeding purposes. Permits are only issued when it can be proved that the animal was legally acquired and that the remaining population will not be harmed by the loss.

Appendix II includes species that are not currently threatened with extinction, but that could easily become so if trade is not carefully controlled. Some common animals are listed here if they resemble endangered species so closely that criminals could try to sell the rare species pretending they were a similar common one. Permits are required to export such animals, with requirements similar to those Appendix I species.

Appendix III species are those that are at risk or protected in at least one country. Other nations may be allowed to trade in animals or products, but they may need to prove that they come from safe populations.

CITES designations are not always the same for every country. In some cases individual countries can apply for special permission to trade in a listed species. For example, they might have a safe population of an animal that is very rare elsewhere. Some African countries periodically apply for permission to export large quantities of elephant tusks that have been in storage for years, or that are the product of a legal cull of elephants. This is controversial because it creates an opportunity for criminals to dispose of black market ivory by passing it off as coming from one of those countries where elephant products are allowed to be exported. If you look up the African elephant, you will see that it is listed as CITES I, II, and III, depending on the country location of the different populations.

Organizations

The human race is undoubtedly nature's worst enemy, but we can also help limit the damage caused by the rapid increase in our numbers and activities. There have always been people eager to protect the world's beautiful places and to preserve its most special animals, but it is only quite recently that the conservation message has begun to have a real effect on everyday life, government policy, industry, and agriculture.

Early conservationists were concerned with preserving nature for the benefit of people. They acted with an instinctive sense of what was good for nature and people, arguing for the preservation of wilderness and animals in the same way as others argued for the conservation of historic buildings or gardens. The study of ecology and environmental science did not really take off until the mid-20th century, and it took a long time for the true scale of our effect in the natural world to become apparent. Today the conservation of wildlife is based on far greater scientific understanding, but the situation has become much more complex and urgent in the face of human development.

By the mid-20th century extinction was becoming an immediate threat. Animals such as the passenger pigeon, quagga, and thylacine had disappeared despite last-minute attempts to save them. More and more species were discovered to be at risk, and species-focused conservation groups began to appear. In the early days there was little that any of these organizations could do but campaign against direct killing. Later they became a kind of conservation emergency service—rushing to the aid of seriously threatened animals in an attempt to save the species. But as time went on, broader environmental issues began to receive the urgent attention they needed. Research showed time and time again that saving species almost always comes down to addressing the

Conservation *organizations range from government departments in charge of national parks, such as Yellowstone National Park (right), the oldest in the United States, to local initiatives set up to protect endangered birds. Here (above) a man in Peru climbs a tree to check on the nest of a harpy eagle discovered near his village.*

problem of habitat loss. The world is short of space, and ensuring that there is enough for all the species is very difficult.

Conservation is not just about animals and plants, nor even the protection of whole ecological systems. Conservation issues are so broad that they touch almost every aspect of our lives, and successful measures often depend on the expertise of biologists, ecologists, economists, diplomats, lawyers, social scientists, and businesspeople. Conservation is all about cooperation and teamwork. Often it is also about helping people benefit from taking care of their wildlife. The organizations involved vary from small groups of a few dozen enthusiasts in local communities to vast, multinational operations.

"FOR THE BENEFIT AND ENJOYMENT OF THE PEOPLE"

CREATED BY ACT OF CONGRESS MARCH 1,1872

THE IUCN

With so much activity based in different countries, it is important to have a worldwide overview, some way of coordinating what goes on in different parts of the planet. That is the role of the International Union for the Conservation of Nature (IUCN), also referred to as the World Conservation Union. It began life as the International Union for the Preservation of Nature in 1948, becoming the IUCN in 1956. It is relatively new compared to the Sierra Club, Flora and Fauna International, and the Royal Society for the Protection of Birds. It was remarkable in that its founder members included governments, government agencies, and nongovernmental organizations. In the

years following the appalling destruction of World War II, the IUCN was born out of a desire to draw a line under the horrors of the past and to act together to safeguard the future.

The mission of the IUCN is to influence, encourage, and assist societies throughout the world to conserve the diversity of nature and natural systems. It seeks to ensure that the use of natural resources is fair and ecologically sustainable. Based in Switzerland, the IUCN has over 1,000 permanent staff and the help of 11,000 volunteer experts from about 180 countries. The work of the IUCN is split into six commissions, which deal with protected areas, policy-making, ecosystem management, education, environmental law, and species survival. The Species Survival Commission (SSC) has almost 7,000 members, all experts in the study of plants and animals. Within the SSC there are Specialist Groups concerned with the conservation of different types of animals, from cats to flamingos, deer, ducks, bats, and crocodiles. Some particularly well-studied animals, such as the African elephant and the polar bear, have their own specialist groups.

Perhaps the best-known role of the IUCN SSC is in the production of the Red Data Books, or Red Lists. First published in 1966, the books were designed to be easily updated, with details of each species on a different page that could be removed and replaced as new information came to light.

By 2010 the Red Lists include information on about 45,000 types of animal, of which almost 10,000 are threatened with extinction. Gathering this amount of information together is a

The IUCN Red Lists *of threatened species are published online and can be accessed at:* *http://www. iucnredlist.org*

huge task, but it provides an invaluable conservation resource. The Red Lists are continually updated and are now available on the World Wide Web. The Red Lists are the basis for the categories of threat used in this book.

CITES

CITES is the Convention on International Trade in Endangered Species of Wild Fauna and Flora (also known as the Washington Convention, since it first came into force after an international meeting in Washington D.C. in 1973). Currently 175 nations have agreed to implement the CITES regulations. Exceptions to the convention include Iraq and North Korea, which, for the time being at least, have few trading links with the rest of the world. Trading in animals and their body parts has been a major factor in the decline of some of the world's rarest species. The IUCN categories draw attention to the status of rare species, but they do not confer any legal protection. That is done through national laws.

Conventions serve as international laws. In the case of CITES, lists (called Appendices) are agreed on internationally and reviewed every few years. The Appendices list the species that are threatened by international trade. Animals are assigned to Appendix I when all trade is forbidden. Any specimens of these species, alive or dead (or skins, feathers, etc.), will be confiscated by customs at international borders, seaports, or airports. Appendix II species can be traded internationally, but only under strict controls. Wildlife trade is often valuable in the rural economy, and this raises difficult questions about the relative importance of animals and people. Nevertheless, traders who ignore CITES rules risk heavy fines or imprisonment. Some rare species—even those with the highest IUCN categories (many bats and frogs, for example)—may have no CITES protection simply because they have no commercial value. Trade is then not really a threat.

The Greenpeace ship, seen here in Antarctica, travels to areas of conservation concern and helps draw worldwide media attention to environmental issues.

WILDLIFE CONSERVATION ORGANIZATIONS

BirdLife International
BirdLife International is a partnership of 60 organizations working in more than 100 countries. Most partners are national nongovernmental conservation groups such as the Canadian Nature Federation. Others include large bird charities such as the Royal Society for the Protection of Birds in Britain. By working together within BirdLife International, even small organizations can be effective globally as well as on a local scale. BirdLife International is a member of the IUCN.
Web site: http://www.birdlife.org

Conservation International (CI)
Founded in 1987, Conservation International works closely with the IUCN and has a similar multinational approach. CI offers help in the world's most threatened biodiversity hot spots.
Web site: http://conservation.org

Durrell Wildlife Conservation Trust (DWCT)
Another IUCN member, the Durrell Wildlife Conservation Trust was founded by the British naturalist and author Gerald Durrell in 1963. The trust is based at Durrell's world-famous zoo on Jersey in the Channel Islands. Jersey was the world's first zoo dedicated solely to the conservation of endangered species. Breeding programs at the zoo have helped stabilize populations of some of the world's most endangered animals. The trust trains conservationists from many countries and works to secure areas of natural habitat to which animals can be returned. Jersey Zoo and the DWCT were instrumental in saving numerous species from extinction, including the pink pigeon, Mauritius kestrel, Waldrapp ibis, St. Lucia parrot, and the Telfair's skink and other reptiles.
Web site: http://durrell.org

Fauna & Flora International (FFI)
Founded in 1903, this organization has had various name changes. It began life as a society for protecting large mammals, but has broadened its scope. It was involved in saving the Arabian oryx from extinction.
Web site: http://www.fauna-flora.org

National Audubon Society
John James Audubon was an American naturalist and wildlife artist who died in 1851, 35 years before the society that bears his name was founded. The first Audubon Society was established by George Bird Grinnell in protest against the appalling overkill of birds for meat, feathers, and sport. By the end of the 19th century there were Audubon Societies in 15 states, and they later became part of the National Audubon Society, which funds scientific research programs, publishes

WILDLIFE CONSERVATION ORGANIZATIONS

magazines and journals, manages wildlife sanctuaries, and advises state and federal governments on conservation issues.
Web site: http://www.audubon.org

Pressure Groups
Friends of the Earth, founded in Britain in 1969, and Greenpeace, founded in 1971 in British Columbia, were the first environmental pressure groups to become internationally recognized. Greenpeace became known for "direct, nonviolent actions," which drew attention to major conservation issues. (For example, campaigners steered boats between the harpoon guns of whalers and their prey.)

The organizations offer advice to governments and corporations, and help those that seek to protect the environment, while continuing to name, shame, and campaign against those who do not.

Royal Society for the Protection of Birds
This organization was founded in the 1890s to campaign against the slaughter of birds to supply feathers for the fashion trade. It now has a wider role and has become Britain's premier wildlife conservation organization, with over a million members. It is involved in international activities, particularly in the protection of birds that migrate to Britain.
Web site: http://www.rspb.org.uk

The Sierra Club
The Sierra Club was started in 1892 by John Muir and is still going strong. Muir, a Scotsman by birth, is often thought of as the founder of the conservation movement, especially in the United States, where he campaigned for the preservation of wilderness. It was through his efforts that the first national parks, including Yosemite,

Sequoia, and Mount Rainier, were established. Today the Sierra Club remains dedicated to the preservation of wild places for the benefit of wildlife and the enjoyment of people.
Web site: http://www.sierraclub.org

World Wide Fund for Nature (WWF)
The World Wide Fund for Nature, formerly the World Wildlife Fund, was born in 1961. It was a joint venture between the IUCN, several existing conservation organizations, and a number of successful businesspeople. Unlike many charities, WWF was big, well-funded, and high profile from the beginning. Its familiar giant panda emblem ranks alongside those of the Red Cross, Mercedes Benz, or Coca-Cola in terms of instant international recognition.
Web site: http://www.wwf.org

GLOSSARY

adaptation Features of an animal that adjust it to its environment; may be produced by evolution—e.g., camouflage coloration

adaptive radiation Where a group of closely related animals (e.g., members of a family) have evolved differences from each other so that they can survive in different niches

alpine Living in mountainous areas, usually over 5,000 feet (1,500 m)

anterior The front part of an animal

arboreal Living in trees

baleen Horny substance commonly known as whalebone and growing as plates in the mouth of certain whales; used as a fringelike sieve for extracting plankton from seawater

biodiversity The variety of species and the variation within them

biome A major world landscape characterized by having similar plants and animals living in it, e.g., desert, rain forest, forest

blowhole The nostril opening on the head of a whale through which it breathes

browsing Feeding on the leaves of trees and shrubs

canine tooth A sharp stabbing tooth usually longer than the rest

carnivore An animal that eats other animals

carrion Rotting flesh of dead animals

cloaca Cavity in the pelvic region into which the alimentary canal, genital, and urinary ducts open

diurnal Active during the day

DNA (deoxyribonucleic acid) The substance that makes up the main part of the chromosomes of all living things; contains the genetic code that is handed down from generation to generation

domestication Process of taming and breeding animals to provide help and useful products for humans

dormancy A state in which—as a result of hormone action—growth is suspended and metabolic activity is reduced to a minimum

dorsal Relating to the back or spinal part of the body; usually the upper surface

ecology The study of plants and animals in relation to one another and to their surroundings

ecosystem A whole system in which plants, animals, and their environment interact

edentate Toothless; also any animals of the order Edentata, which includes anteaters, sloths, and armadillos

endemic Found only in one geographical area, nowhere else

estivation Inactivity or greatly decreased activity during hot weather

eutrophication An increase in the nutrient chemicals (nitrate, phosphate, etc.) in water, sometimes occurring naturally and sometimes caused by human activities, e.g., by the release of sewage or agricultural fertilizers

extinction Process of dying out at the end of which the very last individual dies, and the species is lost forever

feral Domestic animals that have gone wild and live independently of people

fluke Either of the two lobes of the tail of a whale or related animal; also a type of flatworm, usually parasitic

gene The basic unit of heredity, enabling one generation to pass on characteristics to its offspring

gestation The period of pregnancy in mammals, between fertilization of the egg and birth of the baby

harem A group of females living in the same territory and consorting with a single male

herbivore An animal that eats plants (grazers and browsers are herbivores)

hibernation Becoming inactive in winter, with lowered body temperature to save energy. Hibernation takes place in a special nest or den called a hibernaculum

homeotherm An animal that can maintain a high and constant body temperature by means of internal processes; also called "warm-blooded"

inbreeding Breeding among closely related animals (e.g., cousins), leading to weakened genetic composition and reduced survival rates

insectivore Animal that feeds on insects. Also used as a group name for hedgehogs, shrews, moles, etc.

keratin Tough, fibrous material that forms hair, feathers, nails, and protective plates on the skin of vertebrate animals

krill Planktonic shrimps

mammal Any animal of the class Mammalia—warm-blooded vertebrate having mammary glands in the female that produce milk with which it nurses its young. The class includes bats, primates, rodents, and whales

matriarch Senior female member of a social group

metabolic rate The rate at which chemical activities occur within animals, including the exchange of gasses in respiration and the liberation of energy from food

monotreme Egg-laying mammal, e.g., platypus

olfaction Sense of smell

omnivore An animal that eats a wide range of both animal and vegetable food

parasite An animal or plant that lives on or within the body of another (the host) from which it obtains nourishment. The host is often harmed by the association

pelagic Living in the upper waters of the open sea or large lakes

pheromone Scent produced by animals to enable others to find and recognize them

placenta The structure that links an embryo to its mother during pregnancy, allowing exchange of chemicals between them

posterior The hind end or behind another structure

prehensile Capable of grasping

primates A group of mammals that includes monkeys, apes, and ourselves

quadruped Any animal that walks on four legs

ruminant Animals that eat vegetation and later bring it back from the stomach to chew again ("chewing the cud") to assist its digestion by microbes in the stomach

underfur Fine hairs forming a dense, woolly mass close to the skin and underneath the outer coat of stiff hairs in mammals

ungulate One of a large group of hoofed animals such as pigs, deer, cattle, and horses; mostly herbivores

uterus Womb in which embryos of mammals develop

vertebrate Animal with a backbone (e.g., fish, mammal, reptile), usually with skeleton made of bones, but sometimes softer cartilage

viviparous (of most mammals and a few other vertebrates) Giving birth to active young rather than laying eggs

FURTHER RESEARCH

Books

Mammals
Macdonald, David, *The New Encyclopedia of Mammals,* Oxford University Press, Oxford, U.K., 2009

Payne, Roger, *Among Whales*, Bantam Press, U.S., 1996

Reeves, R. R., and Leatherwood, S., *The Sierra Club Handbook of Whales and Dolphins of the World*, Sierra Club, U.S., 1983

Sherrow, Victoria, and Cohen, Sandee, *Endangered Mammals of North America*, Twenty-First Century Books, U.S., 1995

Whitaker, J. O., Audubon Society
Field Guide to North American Mammals, Alfred A. Knopf, New York, U.S., 1996

Wilson, Don E., Mittermeier, Russell A., *Handbook of Mammals of the World Vol 1,* Lynx Edicions, Barcelona, Spain, 2009

Birds
Attenborough, David, *The Life of Birds*, BBC Books, London, U.K., 1998

BirdLife International, *Threatened Birds of the World*, Lynx Edicions, Barcelona, Spain and BirdLife International, Cambridge, U.K., 2000

del Hoyo, J., Elliott, A., and Sargatal, J., eds., *Handbook of Birds of the World Vols 1 to 15,* Lynx Edicions, Barcelona, Spain, 1992–2010

Dunn, Jon, and Alderfer, Jonathan K., *National Geographic Field Guide to the Birds of North America,* National Geographic Society, Washington D.C., United States, 2006.

Stattersfield, A., Crosby, M., Long, A., and Wege, D., eds., *Endemic Bird Areas of the World: Priorities for Biodiversity Conservation*, BirdLife International, Cambridge, U.K., 1998

Fish
Buttfield, Helen, *The Secret Lives of Fishes*, Abrams, U.S., 2000

Dawes, John, and Campbell, Andrew, eds., *The New Encyclopedia of Aquatic Life, Facts On File*, New York, U.S., 2004

Reptiles and Amphibians
Corbett, Keith, *Conservation of European Reptiles and Amphibians*, Christopher Helm, London, U.K., 1989

Corton, Misty, *Leopard and Other South African Tortoises,* Carapace Press, London, U.K., 2000

Hofrichter, Robert, *Amphibians: The World of Frogs, Toads, Salamanders, and Newts*, Firefly Books, Canada, 2000

Murphy, J. B., Adler, K., and Collins, J. T. (eds.), *Captive Management and Conservation of Reptiles and Amphibians*, Society for the Study of Amphibians and Reptiles, Ithaca, New York, 1994

Stafford, Peter, *Snakes*, Natural History Museum, London, U.K., 2000

Insects
Eaton, Eric R. and Kaufman, Kenn. *Kaufman Field Guide to Insects of North America*, Houghton Mifflin, New York, U.S., 2007
Pyle, Robert Michael, National Audubon Society *Field Guide to North*

American Butterflies, Pyle, Robert Michael, A. Knopf, New York, U.S., 1995

General
Allaby, Michael, *A Dictionary of Ecology*, Oxford University Press, New York, U.S., 2010

Douglas, Dougal, and others, *Atlas of Life on Earth*, Barnes & Noble, New York, U.S., 2001

Web sites
http://www.nature.nps.gov/ U.S. National Park Service wildlife site

http://www.ummz.lsa.umich-edu/ umich.edu/ University of Michigan Museum of Zoology animal diversity web. Search for pictures and information about animals by class, family, and common name

http://www.cites.org/ CITES and IUCN listings. Search for animals by order, family, genus, species, or common name. Location by country and explanation of reasons for listings

http://www.cmc-ocean.org Facts, figures, and quizzes about marine life

www.darwinfoundation.org/ Charles Darwin Research Center

http://www.fws.gov.endangered Information about endangered animals and plants from the U.S. Fish and Wildlife Service, the organization in charge of 94 million acres of wildlife refuges

http://www.endangeredspecie.com
Information, links, books, and publications about rare and endangered species. Also includes information about conservation efforts and organizations

*http://*www.ewt.org.za Endangered South African wildlife

http://forests.org/ Includes forest conservation answers to queries

http://www.iucn.org Details of species, IUCN listings, and IUCN publications. Link to online Red Lists of threatened species at: www.iucnredlist.org

http://www.panda.org World Wide Fund for Nature (WWF). Newsroom, press releases, government reports, campaigns. Themed photogallery

http://www.pbs.org/journeytoamazonia The Amazonian rain forest and its unrivaled biodiversity

http://wdcs.org/ Whale and Dolphin Conservation Society site. News, projects, and campaigns. Sightings database

INDEX

Words and page numbers in **bold type** indicate main references to the various topics.